What Educators are Saying About *Let the Child Shine!*

The past ten of my thirteen years of teaching have been with preschoolers in the Ferguson-Florissant School District in Ferguson, Missouri. In *Let the Child Shine*, Dr. Scott lays out a pedagogy that affirms my practice of understanding, respecting, and teaching the whole child. What I value most about this book is the metaphorical mirror Dr. Scott put in front of my daily interaction with—and impact on—young children. This book is a wonderful guide to how children develop their "treasures" at each life stage and how educators can help mine and shine (or dim and dull) those treasures. *Let the Child Shine* is a beautiful explanation and celebration of the young child and empowers teachers to do the immeasurably important job of cultivating young hearts and minds.

~Kara Grice
Pre-K Teacher
Ferguson, MO

As a teacher and grandmother, I found Dr. Scott's second book, *Let the Child Shine*, offered me more great information and useful tools to help kids "sparkle." Just like in her first book on the **7 Childhood Treasures** (*Just Be Your S.E.L.F.*, which is helpfully summarized in this new book), she makes child development and learning easy to understand, and I can implement practical strategies immediately. Her Cornerstone Strategies of the Seek Sparkle & Shine Plan for teaching have helped me slow down and tune in more to the children; to see them, not a mini-me, when I look at them; to see this unique child, in this unique moment; to be new and brave in my authenticity with children; and to stay sane, being my best self when I am around children. Dr. Scott's writing is refreshing, enlightening, and inviting to any reader who also desires to treat children with best practices to replace past ineffective practices. She does not make one feel guilty, though, for having said and done things to dim a child's light. I no longer need to call a child "cute" when what I see is their brilliance!

~Rebecca Nottingham
Special Education Teacher
Keystone Learning Services
Ozawkie, KS

Let the Child Shine lets readers reflect on how their own story contributes to the story they write about the children they care for. Dr. Scott lets us see how our childhood story can be both a contributor and an inhibitor to our work with young children. She allows us to gain a different perspective, seeing past the "black-and-white" movie ingrained within us. Instead, she offers her "unique set of lenses to see children [and their work] in technicolor." Though she reminds us of the missteps we sometimes make when caring for young children, she also affirms that neither we nor the children need to be perfect. The fundamental work of teachers is to relish the moment with them!

~Amy Peterson-Roper
School Support Coach
ME Department of Education
and Pre-K—4 Principal (retired)
Ellsworth Elementary Middle School
Ellsworth, ME

Teaching to the Brilliance in a Young Child

L. Carol Scott, PhD

Let the Child Shine
Teaching to the Brilliance in a Young Child
Dr. L. Carol Scott, PhD
Big Dream Press

Published by Big Dream Press, St. Louis, MO
Copyright ©2019 Dr. L.Carol Scott, PhD
All rights reserved.

No part of this publication may be reproduced, stored in a retrieval system, or transmitted in any form or by any means, electronic, mechanical, photocopying, recording, scanning, or otherwise, except as permitted under Section 107 or 108 of the 1976 United States Copyright Act, without the prior written permission of the Publisher. Requests to the Publisher for permission should be addressed to Permissions Department, Big Dream Press at carol @lcarolscott.com

Limit of Liability/Disclaimer of Warranty: While the publisher and author have used their best efforts in preparing this book, they make no representations or warranties with respect to the accuracy or completeness of the contents of this book and specifically disclaim any implied warranties of merchantability or fitness for a particular purpose. No warranty may be created or extended by sales representatives or written sales materials. The advice and strategies contained herein may not be suitable for your situation. You should consult with a professional where appropriate. Neither the publisher nor author shall be liable for any loss of profit or any other commercial damages, including but not limited to special, incidental, consequential, or other damages.

Editor: Karen Tucker, Commaqueenediting.com

Proofreader: Angela Houston, Ahjoyediting.com

Cover and Interior design: Davis Creative, DavisCreative.com

Library of Congress Cataloging-in-Publication Data

Library of Congress Control Number: 2019916722

Dr. L. Carol Scott, PhD

Let the Child Shine: Teaching to the Brilliance in a Young Child

ISBN: 978-1-7326452-2-6

Library of Congress subject headings:

    1. DU023000 – EDUCATION/Early Childhood   2. EDU010000 – EDUCATION/Elementary   3. FAM016000 – FAMILY & RELATIONSHIPS/Education

    2019

ATTENTION CORPORATIONS, UNIVERSITIES, COLLEGES, AND PROFESSIONAL ORGANIZATIONS: Quantity discounts are available on bulk purchases of this book for educational, gift purposes, or as premiums for increasing magazine subscriptions or renewals. Special books or book excerpts can also be created to fit specific needs. For information, please contact Big Dream Press, PO Box 1122, Maryland Heights, MO 63043; ph 866.665.5569.

For you, teacher. Just for you.

Acknowledgments

I thank my mother for her role model as a teacher with a passion for education. My love of teaching began with witnessing my mother's love of teaching. Like she had, though, I "fell" into my career in education quite unintentionally. Also like Mom's, my enthusiasm as an educator grew with each year of practice and learning. Thank you, Mom.

I am deeply grateful to the internationally respected University of Kansas faculty who exposed me to Froebel, Dewey, Montessori, Piaget, Vygotsky, Bruner, and other developmental theorists and researchers, as I earned a BA, MA, and PhD in the Department of Human Development and Family Life. My teachers from those years are too numerous to name.

To hundreds of children and their families, across three university-based children's centers, I am forever indebted. During my years of university study and early career, I also taught and supervised in university preschools. To you parents, grands, enrolled children, and siblings, thank you for adding to my "book learning" with a daily, invaluable laboratory on how development prospers and is hindered.

For significant influence on my thinking about pedagogy, and on my understanding of good educational environments for young children, I am intellectually indebted to Sam Meisels, Judy Jablon, Cathy Fosnot, Constance Kamii, and Rheta DeVries, along with several colleagues who were also members of the national faculties for the *Project Construct Curriculum Framework* and the *Work Sampling System*.

I am grateful to Dr. Jim Caccamo, then of the Independence Missouri School District, and to the federal Office of Head Start for the opportunity to work in public schools with teachers, children, and families in K–3. This experience brought three powerful new additions to my teacher toolkit: Sylvia Chard and Lillian Katz's Project Approach, Malaguzzi's Reggio Emilia approach, and the strengths-based model for supporting children and families.

I am deeply grateful to the generosity of the Ewing Marion Kauffman Foundation and the leadership of Dr. Stacie Goffin for the funding of initiatives to bring national innovators to speak to early learning professionals in the Kansas City metropolitan area. During the boom of national press on early brain development in the late 1990s, I learned directly from Pediatric Neurologist Harry Chugani, author of the earliest PET scan studies. Long before our current understanding of the impacts of Adverse Childhood Experiences, thanks to Dr. Goffin's forward thinking, I learned about early trauma from Dr. Bruce Perry. Now senior fellow at the Child Trauma Academy in Houston, Perry was speaking then on his analysis of trauma in the children of the Waco siege of 1993.

Many similar experiences and choice learning opportunities throughout my career have been integrated into my current understanding of how to support children's development from birth through age seven. I am grateful for them all.

I am grateful for a lifestyle that allows me to sit for hours, fingers on keyboard, musing out what I know from a forty-year career that may be of value to teachers of children from birth through age seven. These past few years, I have been blessed by time to integrate all these learning opportunities of my career into my best advice on social and emotional development.

Once all the words were written, the next steps on the way to a book brought more openings for gratitude. For excellence in copy editing, I

Acknowledgments

thank Karen Tucker, of Comma Queen Editing, who blessed me with exactly the level of tough love a writer like me needs and also many new bits and bobs of arcane punctuation and grammar knowledge. For inventive layout and cover design, and a beyond-comfortable partnership, I am grateful to Cathy and Jack Davis of Davis Creative. Angela Houston, of A.H. Joy Editing, helped ensure the correct final arrangements of letters and lines with her outstanding proofreading. As she focused like a laser on the final details, she also enjoyed the content. Such dual attention is a rare gift! Thank you to everyone who made this book a dream come true.

Table of Contents

Acknowledgments vii
Introduction 1
What Do We Really Want for Children? 7
    Are You Willing to See in a New Way? 8
    Children Arrive with Sparkle! 9
    How Do Kids Sparkle? 11
    How Bright Can They Be? 11
    How Do We Dull Their Shine? 13
    Why Adults Aren't Cute 15
The Anti-Sparkle Plan 19
    Patronizing Passerby 20
    Smooth Operator 23
    Wild Child Tamer 26
    Professor Fear 29
    I Am the Boss of You 32
    Don't Feel Bad, Okay? 38
    See Their Brilliance 40
Cornerstone Strategies of the Seek Sparkle & Shine Plan 45
    #slowdowntunein – Slow Down, Tune In 45
    #seethemnotyou – See Them, Not You 50
    #thischildthismoment – This Child, This Moment 52

#benewbebrave – Be New, Be Brave 54

#staysanebeyourself – Stay Sane, Be Your S.E.L.F. 57

The "Short Course" 61

Your Little Red House and C.A.R. 61

Individuation: A Life Journey 62

The 7 Childhood Treasures 64

Treasure-Centered Teaching 67

The Dynamics of Mining Trust. 68

Broken Tools. 69

Basic Tools 72

Discovering the Boundaries of Independence 75

Broken Tools. 80

Basic Tools 85

The Explosion of Faith 89

Broken Tools. 91

Basic Tools 94

Negotiation by the Boxes. 96

Broken Tools. 101

Basic Tools 104

The Vision and the Plan. 114

Broken Tools. 115

Basic Tools 118

Release to Compromise	122
Broken Tools	124
Basic Tools	126
Persistence via Acceptance	130
Broken Tools	132
Basic Tools	134
Educating in the Little Red House	139
Conclusion	143
About the Author	145

Introduction

This Book is for Teachers. I have written this book expressly for the audience of teacher-caregivers for children from birth through seven years of age. No matter the environment in which you care for and educate a group of children, whether in a family child care home, Head Start or other preschool, child care center, public or private PK–3 or K–6 school, if your role is teacher, this book is for you. Thank you, from the depths of my heart, for the crucially important and highly impactful work you do!

I recognize that this audience is extremely diverse. It includes staff in child care programs who, in some states, have no training or education to prepare them for teaching young children. They may know little to nothing at all about child development. This readership also includes public school pre-K to second grade teachers, each of whom holds at least a baccalaureate degree, if not a master's, in elementary or early childhood education. Even so, I recognize that schools of education have not traditionally infused their teacher training programs with information on child development, so even many of those readers have limited knowledge or understanding about early development.

I assume that the developmental range for this readership is as broad as that for a classroom full of young children, and each of you knows what THAT is like! Acknowledging this diversity, my goal was to write in a way that would work for everyone. My language and message have not been, I believe, diminished to create accessibility for those who come to this work without a high school diploma. (Missouri child care regulation, for example, only requires staff in licensed centers and preschools to be eighteen years old and free of tuberculosis, though individual programs may have higher standards for their hires.) I hope I have made my explanations using lay language suitable for these readers without oversimplifying for those with college education or substantial professional development on the subject of children's emotional and social development.

Maybe Parents Too. So much of what teachers and parents need to know is the same or similar when it comes to having authentic relationships with children. The **Cornerstone Strategies** and **Basic Tools** presented here for teachers can work for, or be adapted to home and family life, by those who are willing…at least, until I write a book especially for parents!

Reality Caveat. As you read, three questions may come to mind. One, are these stories and examples of children and teachers real? Two, is this Basic Tool one Dr. Scott has used as a teacher, and has it been found effective? Three, is there a foundation of pedagogical practice and research under these strategies and tools? I'm giving you the answers right up front.

One—Yes, the child stories are real. Often, I am directly quoting a child or describing actions of a child I taught or knew in some other non-classroom situation. However, not all these stories are about real *individuals*. In some examples, the behavior I describe or words I "quote" are a blend of my experiences with several children. These are age-typical generalizations based on actual children. These examples give you my experiences with children, filtered through the lens of a career developmental psychologist. The result is a kaleidoscope image, which pieces together bits of behavior by real children, to create a mosaic of a "universal child" of that age.

Also, examples of teacher classroom behavior are real. Many come directly from my own past as a teacher (I tell on myself a lot), or I witnessed them in other teachers during my career. But no, I was not a direct witness of all that I describe. Some examples I repeat from teachers who attended one of my workshops or coaching sessions, describing their own behavior or that of a colleague. Other stories were told by expert speakers I have heard or were documented in images and shared quotes in sessions in which I was a learner. So, some stories have been through the filters of another observer before I added my filters. No doubt, they were somewhat altered by each set of filters.

That said, a major source of this "oral history" was my work on the faculties of both the Project Construct National Center and the Work Sampling System in the 1990s. In these teacher-educator roles, I benefited from a wealth of professional development offered by national thought leaders in constructivist education. This bounty exponentially expanded from the additions of experience and expertise shared by the teachers who attended the PCNC and WSS institutes.

Finally, relative to the reality of the child and teacher stories you will read in these pages, as project director for a federally funded research project, I received an intensive education in the world-renowned Reggio Emilia approach. I am grateful to have learned about Reggio directly from a visiting Italian team, comprised of an *insegnante* (teacher), *atelierista* (creative resource director), and *pedagogista* (educational psychologist and principal). Their beautifully documented stories of children's learning made me a witness, at a distance, to a unique system of education. The Reggio Emilia approach invokes a brilliance in young children we rarely get to see here in the United States, and I think we need more of that shine!

Sadly, for me, relative to the second question, many of these adult learning experiences blessed my career long after I had transitioned from classroom teacher to administrator and CEO. So, I have continuously searched out opportunities to observe other teachers using these teaching strategies or to field-test these tools on any children in non-classroom or pseudo-classroom (e.g., Sunday school) settings. I have added those strategies, tools, and approaches that I saw improve the authentic relationship between adult and child to my teaching of teachers.

The **Broken Tools** are all real examples of what doesn't work. I believe many readers will have witnessed most, if not all, of them if they're being honest. In fact, most readers will see themselves in many of the Broken Tools. Looking in a mirror is hard sometimes, but we'll get through it together. And no, these tools were not all exhibited by real individuals either. As with the children stories, to make a point, sometimes I have created blends from multiple teachers with similar experiences across four decades of working with and observing teachers and parents.

So, the answer for the second question is yes but also no because the Basic Tools I describe are a mixture: some are tried and tested and known to be effective, while some are—let us say—aspirational. However, this no is tempered by the answer to the third and final question you may have pondered.

That answer is yes, there is a rigorous foundation of pedagogical practice and research under these Basic Tools, even if not every idea has been tried and tested in a classroom. Most have, and the rest are developmentally aligned with expectations for the age group. They incorporate evidence-informed teaching practices. They are similar to activities I've observed or learned about from teachers that *have* been tried and tested.

Truly, I'm hoping some of you readers who are in classrooms right now will try those Basic Tools that are my hopeful creations. Help me take them to that next step of confirmation. Field-test any of the Basic Tools within your classroom community and let me know how they work for you!

Introduction

Grammar Note. In all my past writing, I have used either a grammatical convention for gender codified in a style manual or my own feminist take on escaping the male default (which uses "he" for any person). Either I avoided gender through the plural (children/they) or alternated between male and female pronouns, sometimes sentence by sentence (first she/her then, in the next sentence, he/him).

In this book, I have chosen to adopt a new convention to honor what is emerging in our ever-changing language. Within the latest generations, the perception of gender has become more fluid, with more individuals preferring not to identify as one of two binary genders and asking for the use of they/them as a preferred personal pronoun rather than a gender-specific pronoun. I have adopted a new strategy, based on this cultural practice, to replace my former convention of alternating two genders with *they* and *them* becoming singular pronouns. I ask the strict grammarians among my readers, who adhere to style manual rules or their elementary school grammar lessons, to forgive me. I hope you can relax into the prose stream, even though it may occasionally splash up into your nose and make you splutter.

My intention is not to disrespect the style manuals but to honor our social and language evolutions as best I can. I'd rather jump on board than stand in front of a series of trains heading for our future. (In the end, I guess I simply don't want to be one of *those* older people!) Still, for me, use of singular verbs with they/them is like nails on a chalkboard, so I continue to use plural verbs in those sentences in which "they/them" is used to indicate "a child."

What Do We Really Want for Children?

What do you want for the children in your charge?

As a teacher, my bottom line is wanting children to go forth from my tender care into a life in which they avoid serious injury and illness, incarceration, addictions, and poverty. Beyond those basics, I want to see them shine in every way possible! I want them to make the best use possible of their minds and hearts as they achieve some understanding of life in all its complexities. I hope for them a productive life, blessed by work and family. Sometimes I dream of their future happiness.

As a teacher, I wish children a long life of experiences shared with others, in relationships that fulfill different aspects of who they are. I dream of a world for them populated with friends, sweethearts, coworkers, and like-minded comrades in both spiritual and civic communities. I want their lives to bring joyful challenges and growth, creating happy memories. I dream of a firm foundation that enables continued generativity in the final years of their lives. I hope for them a connection to a higher power, with some sense of guidance from a divine source.

If I'm completely honest, I also hope they expand *my* life experiences with the pleasure of pride in their successes and their outputs—whether through bringing their own children into the world, earning diplomas, building fine careers, creating meaningful art, or living in faith. What teacher doesn't love to hear, decades later, from a former student whose life we touched with meaning?

How does this sound to you as a teacher? Am I close to your mark? Would you say no to any of that for a child you teach? Could you turn down any of those pursuits for a child you are charged to protect, nurture, and educate? You want those children for whom you are responsible to be well and happy, yes? You want them to enjoy their lives, right? Preferably, they should never suffer. And you want them to SHINE!

What if you could have a significant role in ensuring they do? Except for the guarantee of never suffering, these imagined children *are* possible. In fact, the bedrock matrix for a shiny **Sparkle Kid** lives within every child from birth. Each child is born with all the raw ores needed. Every single child. We early childhood teachers have the joy of helping them unpack all that.

I apologize for being this blunt, but we adults—teachers and parents, both—are also the ones who mess up that "original" kid. We don't mean to, but we do.

Are You Willing to See in a New Way?

I'm willing to bet that, as a professional educator, you want to see in your classroom what I call **Sparkle Kids**. Sometimes, though, even as young as two years, all we can see in this still-innocent newcomer to our world is the pain from a heap of life experiences that have already been piled on.

Unfortunately, we tend to further bury those children's lights. We do. These children, who have not yet begun to shine, are often disruptive and annoying and sometimes painful to be around. And so, we pile on more layers of pain and further dim that light.

We must look harder into these children to see the shine through the dim shell of an already hardening heart. The light is innate, part of their hard wiring. It is still there, no matter how old the child. It is never too late for anyone. As one example, when I finally started digging out at age thirty, only the dimmest sparks were visible, buried under an impossibly deep heap of early trauma and subsequent self-sabotaging life experiences.

This book invites you into a new way of seeing all children. As a fellow teacher and early learning professional, I offer you a unique set of lenses to see children's social and emotional development in Technicolor®. Maybe after years of seeing children only as sepia-toned, blurry versions of their true glory, you are about to be surprised. Maybe you've been seeing flashes of color for years, wondering how to bring them out and brighten them up.

I've witnessed what happens whenever a teacher opens a channel of authentic, full-color relationship with a child. These openings can happen at three months, three years, thirteen, or beyond. Children whose Sparkle Kids are honored in authentic relationships become fully themselves rather than stunted caricatures or restrictive roles. Children who are encouraged to be fully themselves, unique and powerful—while also developing a community conscience—grow into successful happy adults who thrive in their relationships.

That's what you want for all the children you teach, yes? To fully see the shine of them and bring it into full, blazing glory? In this book, we find that shine at its source: at two days; one year; two, three, and four years; five, six, and seven years.

Children Arrive with Sparkle!

In my first book, *Just Be Your S.E.L.F.—Your Guide to Improving Any Relationship*, I described early developmental pathways for the social and emotional assets needed to achieve great relationship skills as an adult. From birth to seven years, each child is meant to find their interpersonal brilliance in the form of *7 Childhood Treasures*: Trust, Independence, Faith, Negotiation, Vision, Compromise, and Acceptance.

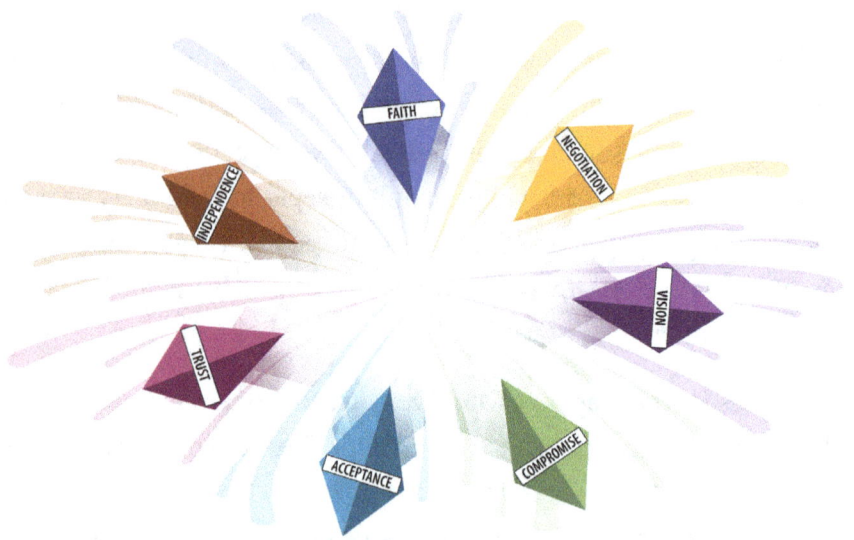

These are the seven ways in which a child, any child—including you, when you were a child—shines from birth. The raw ores of these gemstones shimmer in the depths of each child, ready for the mining work that will bring them into the light, cut their facets to fully develop their brilliance, and polish them to a subtle luster.

We teachers provide tools needed for the job, and because this imagery is one big metaphor, those tools are not hammers and drills but interpersonal interactions. Children don't get to mine their **Childhood Treasures** because of the board games we buy them or the apps they play with. The Treasures are mined during social engagement—which, for the first three years, occurs mostly with us grown-ups!

How Do Kids Sparkle?

I always know a Sparkle Kid when I see one. They're lively, present, and engaged. Even when incapable of speech, they're eager to communicate, confident that their interests will be welcomed, considered, and taken seriously. They notice the world around them with concentration, explore it with curiosity, and pursue their interests with probing questions. They are voracious learners, slurping up the luxuriously abundant and tasty world in excited gulps, savoring every new tang and texture. I can see this shine as early as a few days old.

By age five, these Sparkle Kids live happily in their own skins, asking for what they need and want with ease and confidence. By age eight, a Sparkle Kid easily accepts most of the Nos in life. Some, at this still-modest age, are even resilient enough to stay upright in the wind tunnel of life, blasted by forces such as bullying at school or parental drama at home.

How Bright Can They Be?

If we stay out of the kids' way, and offer competent support, then Sparkle Kids can have the following capacities by the time they are eight years old:

- Getting their basic relationship needs met by trusting others in healthy ways.
- Knowing and feeling comfortable with who they are uniquely—physically, mentally, emotionally, and energetically—and with this uniqueness in others.
- Belief in miracles, Big Dreams that come true, and fanciful wishes fulfilled.
- Getting what they want and helping others get what they want in a win-win approach to life.

- Competent goal setting and achieving of goals that matter to them and their communities.
- Surrendering selfishness to help create a world that works for everyone.
- Carrying on with resilience, rising again after a fall; moving through pain, sorrow, regret, fear, and anger as easily as through joy, love, connection, and peace.

Are you surprised that these attributes might all be gathered together in one smallish eight-year-old child? Do you believe children of this age are too young for these sophistications?

Perhaps you never met such a child, and that would not surprise me. Unfortunately, here in the United States, they are rare. Most of our families, early care and education programs, and K–12 schools have not been stellar at fostering Sparkle Kids.

That's tough to hear, I know, especially as a teacher, and you may feel the need to defend yourself. This truth doesn't mean that you are a bad teacher, and actually, there's easy confirmation of my statement: How many adults do you know who carry all those competencies listed above? Read the list again and think of who you know like that. Not too many, I'm guessing.

And why is that? The answer is exactly what you might expect, given your choice of profession as an early care and education professional. For far too many of us, life's early experiences fostered the opposite of every item on that list. Early learning—early experience that wires the brain—determines who we become. So, if we're not turning out many people with these assets, where do we go wrong?

How Do We Dull Their Shine?

"Children are so cute!"

I hear or read some version of this statement almost every day. You probably do too. I even hear adults say it directly to children, or about them, when they're within earshot. "You are so cuh-yoot!!" is a common response to a child. Similarly, "Aren't they cute?" is a routine observation of children playing or talking together.

> **Any Child:** *[awkward silence]* "Um…I'm right here, you know, living an internal life just as complex as yours…And I can hear you."

As a developmental psychologist, I am plagued by "cute." Far beyond the level of personal pet peeve, my concern is that our overuse of this label limits our ability to see the amazing sparkle in children that is *so much more* than cute. I fear that, as a label, "cute" often disrespects—even, dismisses—who a child really is. Yes, even an infant.

Let's try an imaginary scenario from *your* life as a teaching tool. I invite you to imagine the following interaction: You have just passionately expressed your strongly held opinion on a subject you are discussing with your spouse/significant other. They reply, in a high-pitched and sing-song voice, "You are SOOOO cuh-yoot when you're angry!!"

How are you feeling about that? Respected? Seen for your competence?

Here's another adult scenario to consider. You are surprised at your birthday party by a special guest—a beloved childhood friend whom you haven't seen in years—and you both begin to cry as you look into each other's eyes for a moment of tender, bittersweet reunion. As you feel your intense emotional connection and sorrow for all the missed years begin to flood out your eyes, the friends and family around you begin a chorus of, "Ooooooh! Aren't they cute? Quick! Somebody get a picture!"

How are you liking that interpretation of your authentic moment of loving reunion? Do you feel emotionally supported? Emotionally safe?

One more example, if you will, of turning our "cute kids" dynamic around on the adult world: With extreme and intense focus, you are struggling to learn a new skill. A do-it-yourself video playing on your phone, you are handling unfamiliar tools, taking a bit of a risk with a household appliance. Chewing on your lower lip, you frown at the video and blow a raspberry at the screen. Your older sibling comments, "Aren't you cute there with your little tools? Awwwww!"

Please, restrain yourself from fratricide. Truly, though, doesn't this scenario rile you up a bit? If not, at least can you admit that you feel less connected to your sibling right now, more distant rather than closer?

In the context of two adults interacting, it's so much easier to see the disrespect, isn't it? Can you see how that label of "cute" minimizes or even erases the targeted person's meaningful experience?

Now, please don't get me wrong. I understand cute, and, yes, young children do trigger the "Awwwww!" response in me too. And, heck, even *I'm* cute! Adorable, some say. <wink> And that's my wrinkling, aging self!

See? Cute has a broad definition and varied synonyms to match our intentions in such observations of children: attractive and pretty, delightful and charming, endearing and lovable, adorable and darling, sweet and appealing. Children can certainly be all those things (and certainly, let's liberally apply this more varied vocabulary to them), AND they are so much more than all those synonyms.

My experience is that we adults over-apply our explosive, "Oh SO cuh-yoot!!" response. We especially do so in situations in which something important is going on with a child about which we feel uncomfortable. Highly focused moments of intense learning or deeply felt emotion, when a child's brilliance is shining like a beacon, may hold too much intimacy for us to bear. Or we simply don't know how to respond in the moment. So, we lump those moments in with the Cupid's bow mouths, big eyes, dimply smile, and bubbling laughter as simply "cute." When we do that, we miss a child's brilliance, how they sparkle in one hundred thousand ways, beyond being easy on the eye and charming.

Why Adults Aren't Cute

The mantle of cuteness is not usually applied to adults in such an across-the-board manner because we adults tend to take each other more seriously more of the time. We believe other adults are our peers, with capacities, value, and self-awareness roughly equivalent to ours—some a little more so, some a little less.

We usually believe adults' statements about their emotions. We respect or at least listen to their thoughts and ideas (even wild conspiracy theories) and honor their spiritual and religious beliefs, even if they're quite different from ours. If a friend said to you, "I truly believe my work is guided by a divine purpose," you would be unlikely to reply, "Oh, that is soooo CUTE!" Yet a three-year-old's statement, "God told me I need a baby brother!" might very well be so labeled.

To me, there is no difference between the two statements. I respect them equally. I believe them equally. Of course, if the three-year-old says God will turn their baby brother into a giraffe, I don't believe it the same way. Yet I *will* still take it seriously as an external expression of something real and important inside this little person. I will not laugh, unless they make it clear they are joking, or call them cute. I will be curious and ask questions to learn more.

Young children sparkle with characteristics such as intelligence, curiosity, tenderness, passion, forcefulness, thoughtfulness, humor, innovation, creativity, and so many more. In this, they are like adults. These little beings, from birth, have a mind, heart, and spirit significant enough to be taken seriously by adults.

Certainly, children's expressions of these various forms of brilliance do not look like our expressions. That is, a child's curiosity, forcefulness, and humor manifest differently from how these characteristics show up in adults. We need to learn to see their shine with different eyes than we see our own. Yet their expressions are as real and valid as ours.

When you label children as cute, over and over, failing to name all their forms of brilliance, you take them out of their humanity and place them in a role. Their behavior—which originated as an expression of what they think, feel, and long for—has now become a little scripted play for your entertainment and enjoyment.

Now they do what they do so you will be pleased and call them cute. They begin to live for your applause and praise rather than your awareness of who they are inside. When I see this pattern happening for a child, it fills me with grief. The loss of talent to the world is incalculable.

Brilliance is complicated, though. Perhaps we dismiss it because—and we must admit this—brilliance is not always as pleasing as cuteness. Children's brilliance can challenge adults. It can scare us when it seems greater than our own. It can confront us and wake us up to our own empty chatter, to the roles we are playing, to how we hide our own lights.

When we can get beyond our *cute* filter and see every child's brilliance, suddenly everything changes. What children do doesn't change. The meaning they are making doesn't change. *You* change. You suddenly see.

Yes, I am writing this book to change you. My hope is that this little book opens your eyes wider to see beyond the cuteness of young children to their sparkle, the shiny brilliance every child brings into the world. My secret plan is to lure you into more authentic relationships with children.

First, you have to see clearly all the other ways we dim the natural shine in a child. Oh, yes…there's more than Cuteness Syndrome.

The Anti-Sparkle Plan

(aka How to Bury the Sparkle Kid in any Child)

Certainly, if a child is experiencing **Adverse Childhood Experiences (ACEs)**, then their sparkle is getting buried. Researchers have shown these ACEs lead to long-term negative health and behavioral outcomes in adults. Yet many children have never experienced one of these ACEs and still lost their sparkle, so how does *that* happen?

> **Adverse Childhood Experiences (ACEs)**
> - Physical abuse
> - Emotional abuse
> - Sexual abuse
> - Domestic violence
> - Parental substance abuse
> - Mental illness (including postpartum depression)
> - Suicide or death
> - Crime or imprisoned family
> - Continuous stress from poverty, illness, or disability

The most common source of what I refer to as the Anti-Sparkle Plan is not ACEs but what I have labeled **MODs**—moments of **Missed Opportunity Development**. Teachers miss chances every day to hand children the Basic Tools for mining their *7 Childhood Treasures*. Sometimes we hand them Broken Tools that wind up burying the ores for those Treasures ever deeper. Other times, we have no tool to offer because we never mined our own Childhood Treasures. It's almost as if we had a plan to make sure children lose their sparkle.

In fact, we do, though the "plan" is completely subconscious and involuntarily inherited, passed down through the generations intact. I've identified five cornerstones of the Anti-Sparkle Plan. Sadly, it's a sort of pentagon from which we adults unwittingly wage war on children's natural journey of individuation. The whole Anti-Sparkle Plan and most MODs in the classroom come from teachers' overreliance on these five styles of interaction:

- Patronizing Passerby
- Smooth Operator
- Wild Child Tamer
- Professor Fear
- I Am the Boss of You

Before you wonder whether you've been any of these, what do these terms even mean? I promise they are simple to understand with only a little explanation. You'll recognize them immediately, either in your own behavior as a teacher, in the remembered behavior of your parents or teachers, in the observed behavior of others outside your immediate family, or even in stylized or caricatured versions of adult–child relationships we see in TV shows and movies. These are archetypes that are literally everywhere in our culture.

Please don't feel too badly that some or all of these styles are familiar in your own behavior. At some point in my life, I have leaned heavily on each one. In fact, they describe most or all adults, at least at times. No one is perfect all the time. You came here to learn from a book because you are one of those who always seek new ways, yes? First, it helps to admit to the old ways.

Patronizing Passerby

This archetype is a cousin of neglect. I am not talking about extreme neglect, such as caregiving impeded by alcohol, drugs, or depression. I'm not talking about teachers who still don't know a child's name by the Fall Open House. I'm talking about the benign neglect of adult

The Anti-Sparkle Plan

busyness: being busy as an art form or as palliative care for our own "I'm not enough" self-talk.

We've all been there/done that, failing to take the time for real connection with a child—barking an order from across the room; picking up the pacifier and poking it in a mouth to stop the fussing rather than responding to it; replying "Not now" for the thirteenth time to the kid tugging on your sleeve for attention.

Children need so much from us. They are utterly dependent on us for everything from physical care to intellectual stimulation to management of big emotions. Then they have the audacity to also *want* us for an endless stream of information, attention, decisions, advice, attention, nurture, comfort, attention, learning, calming, protection…and did I mention attention?

I've heard a lot of adults who've chosen early childhood education as a profession—or at least a job—complain about this endless river of demand from children. Yes, children are demanding of your time and attention. Yes, it's endless. Yes, if feels like you could drown sometimes.

I have something very important to say to you about that, and I say it with love and compassion because I've been in your shoes: This is the job. This is what you chose. Responding to that endless stream of needs and wants is what they pay you to do. No, the pay is not enough, but here you are. Suck it up, count to five, and pay attention. No, not to me… to the Sparkle Kid in front of you!

For teachers, the width of this river of children's demands is sometimes wide—up to 35 children wide in K–2 classrooms of underfunded public schools—and the waters in the stream change regularly. New debris in the stream and new forces behind the flood occur year by year with younger children—sometimes even hour by hour—and semester by semester when they get older.

You never know, as a teacher, how many needs across how wide a developmental span you will face as you meet each new group of children. But the job stays the same. You respond to the Sparkle Kids in front of you. You show up for them.

Showing up well, showing up fully, being present to the children as the main attraction while you move the priorities for everything else in your life to the side for a bit…well, that's what makes education a career for the strong of heart, mind, and spirit.

Patronizing Passerby flips this priority, making *everything else* the main attraction, and the children are the side job that takes second or third priority. They're in the way of your paperwork, blocking your hurried snack prep, slowing you down as you clean up the spill, adding more problems and frustrations to your day. They're the "Oh, not now!" and "Oh, not again!" factors more often than "Oh, goody!" and "How delightful!" factors.

It seems odd that this could be true for teachers, yet it is for many. There is so much to do in the modern early learning and K–12 education systems. An astonishingly large percentage of it has nothing to do with supporting children's development. Devastatingly, that extracurricular burden also carries much higher stakes for the teacher. When employment or funding is at risk, it's easy for the kids to be passed by, even at preschool.

Patronizing Passerby behavior ranges along a continuum. At one end is the vacant "uh-huh" muttered periodically to the endlessly talking four-year-old trailing behind you, yammering, while you think about and do twenty-nine other things. At this end of the continuum, we also find actions like popping the drooping pacifier back in the mouth of an infant as you walk by because you know if it drops, the baby will wake, and your free time will end.

At the other end of the continuum is a teacher feeding one toddler with one hand while using the other to dance a toy bear on the high-chair tray of a second child, a whimpering, struggling toddler who is yelling to "GET DOWN!" Interspersed between "Take another bite?" to the first child are little enthusiastic cries of "See the bear, honey?" "Watch the bear dance, okay?" On this end of the continuum, we also find the teacher who, faced with a seven-year-old's fierce grief and anger over losing a soccer game, jocularly suggests, "Hey, it's all okay, right? Ya win some, ya lose some! Whaddya say we turn that frown upside down, eh?"

Here's how I know when I'm being a **Patronizing Passerby**: I'm really not seeing the Sparkle Kid. My attention is truly on something else, and I'm multitasking while on autopilot, and making no real connection in the interaction with the child.

Am I saying that you must always, every waking minute of your time with children, focus 100 percent of your attention on them and do nothing else? Of course not. I recommend you sharpen your focus on a child another 10 to 20 percent and see how that improves their behavior. Maybe you'll decide to sharpen your focus even more.

Smooth Operator

Frankly, in some ways, it's better to be the child who gets at least some passerby attention than to be the one getting this treatment. We adults all do this one, too, all the time. Like an old-style movie projectionist, I am being a **Smooth Operator** when I assume a child is doing something for the same reason I, or another adult, might do it. I project the movie of my motivation onto the child, smoothly running reel after reel of my reality, treating the child as my screen. The examples are plentiful!

One common one is the projected motivation of willfulness in the very young child. When I was an infant, child-rearing lore said that children cried to be picked up as a strategy to control parental attention. Picking up infants and toddlers whenever they cried was believed to "spoil" children, making them badly behaved and demanding. Although less common today, adults still project such willfulness onto infants, toddlers, and older children (see **Wild Child Tamer** below).

Using behavior to label a child also fits into this category. When a fourteen-month-old hides behind their parents' legs when confronted with strangers, they are not shy…until we tell them and the whole world that they are, over and over. In fact, they're experiencing a normal stage of child development in which fear of strangers is strong, from about 8 to 18 months. They'll grow out of it as long as nobody puts them in the "shy" box.

When a three-year-old boy pushes down a girl, apparently just to see them fall and cry, some nearby adult may say, "Oh, look! He likes her!" or "Boys will be boys!" Adult assignment of benign intent, and even affection, as motivation for an aggressive act does no favors for either of these future adults.

A huge minefield of smoothly projected adult motivation lies in children's early sexual development and sexuality. Child care teachers continue the generational transmission of the changing-table message that touching your genitals is "nasty" or "naughty." This type of generationally transmitted body shame is also invoked when we assign sexual intention or motivation onto preschoolers' developmentally normal naptime masturbation or natural curiosity about the genitals of other children. They don't already know what we know about sexuality and the body. They are learning.

Teachers everywhere also struggle with helping children develop the values and morals expected in their community and culture. Most of the struggle results from projecting onto children's behavior our established morals and values. When we project malicious intent onto children's earliest falsehoods, for example, teaching opportunities get lost in our judgment. And, voila, another Missed Opportunity for Development.

Yes, children do need to learn that lying to escape the negative consequences of their action or inaction is considered wrong. They need to learn to self-govern around that. We want them to be unwilling to tell lies because it's wrong rather than because they might get caught. When we call them liars and label some of their early falsehoods as "lies" that merit punishment, we don't teach them not to lie. We simply teach them to be more careful, *to lie better* and avoid getting caught.

Children go through stages of moral development, just as they go through stages of physical, intellectual, social, and emotional development. They develop their understanding of what is right or just over time, like they develop in their ways of thinking, feeling, and apprehending reality. In many ways, children are as different from adults as caterpillars are from butterflies, as tadpoles from frogs. Children don't consume the same reality we do, just like caterpillars do not collect nectar from flowers and tadpoles do not breathe above water.

Even without referencing species that undergo metamorphosis, would the adult tiger assume that the play-fighting of their cubs was comparable in any way with their own adult skills to defend the family? Can you see how this goes badly for children's development? When you project your "King of the Forest" level of understanding onto a cub, what do you assume you no longer need to do to support and protect them? What do you forget to teach them that they don't yet know? In what ways do you become disappointed in their inability to measure up to your assumptions?

Here's how I know when I'm being a **Smooth Operator**: I'm with a child and my mouth is moving. I'm kidding…maybe not. Truly, I find I must be conscious and intentional to stop myself from projecting my ways of understanding and my motivations onto kids.

The key distinction between when I am and when I'm not projecting seems to be as simple and as challenging as the difference between certainty and curiosity, between telling and asking. When I'm certain I know their feelings and telling children how it's going, especially for them, then I'm *very* likely operating my projector. When I'm curious and asking children how it's going, specifically for them, then I am not.

Wild Child Tamer

Let's admit it right up front: toddlers are responsible for this one. I mean, really, do we routinely describe young infants as "wild"? Usually, children begin to seem wild and "terrible" as toddlers, when they're starting to resist our oversight and control of their lives. Essentially, they become annoying when they start to have opinions and interests different from ours, paired with the mobility to independently carry those opinions into action.

Children's prime developmental directive—indeed, their innate imperative—is to **individuate**. This fancy psychology term simply means to become an individual, unique from others. Two-year-olds' roles in the process include discovering the ways in which their needs, wants, feelings, and ideas are different from yours. Their job is to become who they are, not who *you* are or who you think they should be.

Thus, the first word out of most toddlers' mouths is some version of "No!" Someday I will write a toddler–adult translation dictionary, and this one word will have the most definitions. Generally speaking, the diplomatically worded meaning behind a toddler's shouted No is something like, "I'm sure what you want me to do is very interesting and important, but I am deeply engaged right now in examining this object in my hands and I need more time for that."

Beneath a teacher's belief that they must tame a Wild Child is a lack of awareness for children's separate reality. Until three or four years of age, when they can start clearly expressing with speech all the amazing ideas and feelings they have, children can appear to simply not have much going on upstairs. To the uninformed adult, they are "blank slates," it seems. Thus, it becomes the teacher's job, as the grown-up in charge, to fill that toddler slate with the right stuff.

What if we could relax and know that Sparkle Kids create a huge amount of the right stuff themselves *if* we give them the right tools to work with at the right age? We don't need to program brilliance into our children with flash cards and letter-of-the-day curriculums to build their brains.

The very idea makes me laugh aloud! Infants' and toddlers' brains are almost doubling in size, using twice the number of brain cells we adults have, to form billions of new neural connections every day. If fourteen adults spent twenty-four hours transmitting knowledge via direct instruction to one toddler, they could not form more neural connections than the child forms interacting normally with one or two adults.

During this age, brain cells are connecting. That's a fact. Do you want a child's neural network to be wired around black-and-white drawings of faces showing emotions? Or would you prefer to program the infant-toddler neural network around responsive caregiving, gentle touch, kind attention, empathy, compassion, curiosity, and the satisfaction of the urge to explore and learn, all expressed on a real human face?

You get to choose, and please do so knowing that 85 percent of each child's brain is built, connection by connection, from birth to three years. So, flash cards or authentic connection to people and the world: which do you choose?

Our job, as teachers, is not to open the top of the child's head and pour in what they need to know, including all the social standards for behavior. Our *first* job with infants and toddlers, believe it or not, is to provide healthy nutrition to feed that rapidly growing brain. In a newborn, 60 percent of children's calorie intake is committed to the task of doubling the size of the brain. By comparison, we adults feed our brains with only 25 percent of our nutrition. So, first, feed the children well with whole, clean food and a well-balanced diet.

The number two teaching job is to feed the Sparkle Kid's heart, mind, and soul. We support early social and emotional development by supporting the child's mining of the ***7 Childhood Treasures*** with the strategies offered in the next chapter. The strategies I introduce there are largely freely available to anyone. In practice, they often appear as space and freedom to safely explore, respect, time, attention, respect, well-timed conventional information, and—I do not apologize one bit for repeating myself a third time—respect.

Here's how I know when I am acting as the **Wild Child Tamer**: I'm usually in a power struggle with a child, and I'm acting like a child. I blush with shame at the memory of some of the things I have said to children in my younger years. It's difficult to sound like a sane adult when arguing with a preschooler over control of their choice of clothing or whether they should use the bathroom.

Professor Fear

This component of the Anti-Sparkle Plan may be the most grievous. Certainly, it has long-lasting negative effects that are difficult to remedy. As with all these mostly subconscious Anti-Sparkle Plan strategies, it manifests in a range of intensities. Essentially, we teach children to be afraid of things, situations, experiences, and people.

One of the most common and easiest to witness is a teacher's dramatic expression of a phobia to some common object or situation. I've witnessed everything from an aversion to some live creature (especially worms, bugs, spiders, and snakes) and all dead creatures to fear of escalators (field trip), a horror of clowns (ditto), and a resistance to having different foods touch on the meal plate.

Think for a moment on this question, if you will: Where do such fears and aversions come from in you? If you can get past your irrational belief that your own phobias are rational—if you can be rational about this question regarding the origin of your fear—it won't be long before you realize someone must have taught you to be afraid because there is nothing inherently scary or alarming about any of these commonplace items and events. You know how I know? *Millions of people are not afraid of them!*

As you continue to reflect, it won't be much longer before you realize that we often *teach* children to be afraid of these things when they're very small, before they have enough reasoning capacity to question what they're learning. We teach children our fears by modeling our phobias and rationalizing that it's okay to have them. To them, teachers are gods, so of course, they will be affected by every dramatic reaction we have to life.

Apologies if I just offended you, but I stand by what I've written, and I tell you again with love and compassion: You teach the children around you to be afraid of stuff that's silly to be afraid of. Mostly, you do it because the adults in your life did it to you. You could simply stop doing that with a little effort. I think you should make the effort for the sake of the children.

Remember what I wrote about part of the teacher's job being to provide safe exploration and discovery? Children *need* to bring us the bugs, worms, dead things, and spiders they discover, as well as the pretty red leaves, flowers, used condoms, half-empty bags of chips, and (hopefully empty) gin bottles. My advice, no matter what they bring you, is to follow the British maxim, stay calm and carry on. It's the job.

What they bring may depend on your neighborhood, but remember that, regardless of what is in their hands, their experience is always one of discovery, excitement, and learning. They are neither afraid nor disgusted; they are *learning*. Children live, every day, at the cliff's edge of understanding, always leaping off into the space of the unknown in their quest for knowledge. In this, very young children are fearless. They. Will. Touch. Anything. ANY. Thing.

Please match their courage. Be not afraid of the bits of the world they bring you. Rather, use them to teach. Stay calm and say, "That bottle is somebody else's trash. They drank what was in the bottle and then threw it down on the ground when they finished. That's called littering, and it makes our world trashy. It's also getting the dirt and germs from the ground on your hands now. What do you think we should do with the bottle before we wash that dirt and those germs off your hands?" I can think, rather quickly, of five different conversations that could arise from this opening.

There are ways to keep yourself nonreactive to your phobia, such as keeping your distance. Here's an example: "Oh, look! You found a spiderweb covered with lots and lots of baby spiders! Let's stand over here together to look so we don't disturb them." You can also be authentic about it. "Somebody taught me to be afraid of spiders when I was little, so I'm going to stand over here. You know they are not dangerous, so you can look more closely if you want."

Here's the bottom line, my dear fellow teacher: Children's learning shouldn't stop at the edges of your fears. You once experienced them as stop signs for your learning, displayed by some adult's fear, when you were quite small. Please don't let them stop the learning in another generation.

Here's another alternative to simply coping with such fears: Educate yourself. Learn which spiders in your region are dangerous/poisonous and which ones are beneficial. Then pull up your big kid panties and try looking at that spider through the child's wonder. If you can get past your fear, you have free curriculum right in front of you on any number of topics.

More difficult to witness and more painful to endure are the much more subtle and damaging versions of **Professor Fear**, when we teach children to be afraid of life, people, trying, being incorrect, being seen, or of learning itself. When I see children being carefully, if subconsciously, taught that the world is a terrifying place in which they must be constantly on guard, I grieve the loss of future choices they will fail to make. When I see children learning that a person who looks a certain way is not as important as they are, my heart breaks for the future of our world.

I hope the repetition of the same trope will not make it trite, but, once again, if I'm with children and my mouth is moving, I'm probably teaching my fears. Indeed, if I'm awake at all, I may be teaching without talking, for many fears are taught with body language, facial expression, and other forms of nonverbal lessons. Teaching our fears to others is a default setting for most of us and one for which we must cultivate ego-awareness.

To avoid teaching my fears requires awareness, intention, and strength, and I have applied these fiercely to make myself a better teacher. First, to repair the ACEs and MODs of my childhood, I created the Development Do-Overs to mine my own **7 Childhood Treasures**. I have learned to listen to myself and watch myself, as an outside observer might, to notice the ways in which I am teaching my fears to children.

When I spot one, I begin by setting the intention to stop and to change. That intention must be manifested, with strength, through educating myself and changing my behavior. My motivation for these challenging efforts is my understanding of how I limit children's brilliance with my unfounded fears. I simply refuse to pass along the ways my sparkle was dulled when I was a child.

I have learned this lesson: my fears are mine to have and to hold until I release them. They do not belong to the next generation, who will—goodness knows—probably find plenty to fear on their own. They need not start life adopting my fears before they have any emotional or intellectual defense against me.

I Am the Boss of You

This Anti-Sparkle Plan feature should be easiest of all to understand because virtually all of us have experienced it somewhere, at some time, from some authority figure. Whether it was your parents or grandparents, one or more of your teachers, nuns, coaches, a drill sergeant, a work supervisor, or your spouse, you've met someone who was bossy and rule-oriented and spent a lot of time telling you what to do. You've probably witnessed someone using fear, intimidation, threats, punishment, and rewards as tools to manage other people who are seen as less powerful and more dependent, like women, children, and those with different abilities.

The **Boss-of-You** style arises from a model of relationships that says one person must be more powerful than the other, making decisions for that other. This power-over model of interaction says that the person in authority—the teacher—is higher, and the learner is lower in the amount of power they hold. Instruction, teaching, and direction come from the higher-power teacher to the lower-power child in the form of mandates ("Open your book to page 92."), closed choices ("Do you want red paint or blue?"), and nonnegotiables ("No blankies at snack."). Compliance leads to reward and reinforcement. Failure to comply brings a negative condition of punishment in some form.

Sometimes the child receives these mandates graciously and follows them willingly, even eagerly, seeing the teacher as a respected mentor or loving guide. Sometimes the child is antagonistic to the mandates and resists them. The two ends of this continuum for **I Am the Boss** might look like this:

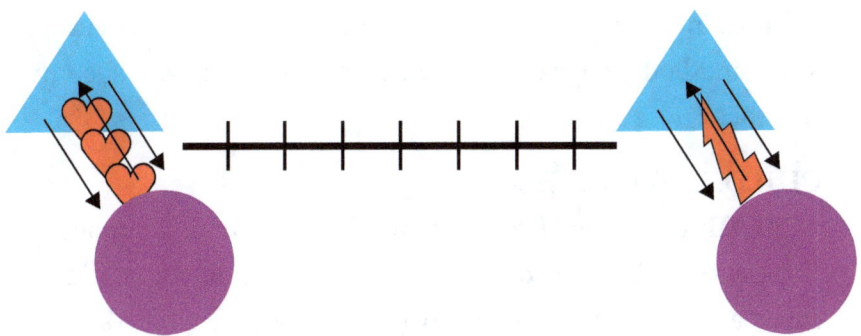

I-Am-the-Boss teachers will find that different children respond differently to this power-over model. Also, the same child, over time, responds differently. They may cooperate sometimes and not others. Some of those variations in compliance and complacency are developmentally driven. Toddlers are natural Boss resisters, as are some preteens and most young teens. The very process of individuation—becoming a unique, individual self—requires resistance to those who boss us.

Some variations in level of cooperation result from the dynamic itself. Authoritarian, power-over models for teaching create resistance because they must violate children's trust. To be a my-way-or-the-highway teacher, I inevitably lie to children. Unfortunately, children have finely tuned B.S. detectors at a very young age. We are caught in our lies and lose children's trust. Remember when you had this experience as a child, learning that a teacher or parent had lied to you to get your cooperation? Over time, some children resist more and more as the adult betrayals mount up.

Another **I-Am-the-Boss** model is found in the way some adults speak to children. The tone I refer to always sounds inauthentic to me. Sometimes it's a little singsongy or overly enthusiastic, sometimes downright smarmy. I wish I could convey the tone and form to you effectively in the written word. When I hear this not-quite-baby-talk tone, I instantly recognize it as a way no adult would ever speak to another adult. You'll have to imagine the voice and the exaggerated silent-film-star facial expressions and body language that sometimes go along with such messages as these:

> **CHILD:** Look what I made.
> **TEACHER:** *[Looking like a wide-eyed "wow" emoji]* Ooooooooo!!! Look at what YOU made! Isn't that special! Well, you are just SO smart and creative, aren't you? *[Clapping]* Yaaaaaaay!! Let's put this beautiful art up here on the board for everyone to admire. Oooooo, child! I'm just so proud of you. Good for you!! *[Turning away in response to a crash in the block area...]*

CHILD: *[Quietly to the retreating adult's back]* Um…I…wasn't…done yet.

This model of control is just one continuous lie, paired with some of the **Patronizing Passerby** model. Our "important" work is getting between us and the truth of children's brilliance. We maintain a veneer, an image of attention, to keep the system running smoothly. If, instead, we were present for the child's experience and striving to share their point of view, the conversation with them might sound more like this:

CHILD: Look what I made.
TEACHER: *[Closely inspecting artwork]* Hey, interesting! Those bright colors make me feel happy. Tell me about it.
CHILD: I'm trying to make all the ways of yellow.
TEACHER: *[Making eye contact and smiling warmly]* I don't understand what you mean. How are you doing that?
CHILD: I'm mixing white in my yellow, first a little, then more and more until a lot. I'm also mixing black in like that too. So, I have a d-d-dark yellow here, with a lot of black, and p-plain yellow here, then, then, then one with lots of white over here. See this one dark yellow here is not so, SO dark as this darker yellow. It has, has, l-less black paint in it. See, I don't know the names of these colors. I am making new colors of yellow, I think, that I can make up names for. Right? *[Big grin!]* But, but, but, I'm not done yet, and I n-n-need more white paint.
TEACHER: *(Responding to crash across the room, continues the conversation while drawing Child along, moving toward the block area.)* That is very interesting to me what you're doing! I'd like to see you finish it, so let me help you get the paint you need. I also know a little bit about where the names of colors come from. Would you like to learn about that?

To me, this conversation rings more authentic and "normal" compared to the first one. It sounds *more* like a conversation between two adults. Of course, we can't say all the things to children we say to adults, nor can we expect them to understand all the vocabulary and concepts we share with adults or even with older children.

Yet we can be *real* with even very young children; we can be authentic. We don't have to speak to them like we're training a teacup Yorkie to jump through embroidery hoops. We can be ourselves. Especially, I believe we *should* each be a S.E.L.F.—Self-governed, Ego-aware, Leading our own life, and Free from the self-imposed barriers (like phobias) we then transmit to the next generation.

The Boss manifests as a range of types too. What I described in the first conversation was the Jocular-Smiling-Cheerleader style of power, which reduces the child to entertainment for us adults. We control the child with our applause and accolades, withholding approval when the child fails to comply with our image of a "good girl" or "good boy." Another style of Boss is the Here's-What-I-Want-Now-Hop-to-It type.

Authoritarian-control-oriented relationships can also manifest much less aggressively, if not much more pleasantly, through dynamics of expectation, guilt, and shame. **The Boss's** control can be backed up with physical punishment, withholding love, nagging, threats of dire consequences, or a points system. The essence is always the same: I'm in charge, and I tell you what to do; your job is to comply. Period.

And—of course—it sometimes absolutely *IS* the teacher's job to tell children, firmly and clearly, the expectations. Helping children develop into community-minded adults who get along in life's sandbox includes sharing standards for behavior.

There is, however, a fundamental difference between helping children learn to make wise choices for their behavior and managing, manipulating, controlling, and bullying children into behaving in ways we prefer. The second-grade teacher who grabbed a child's cheeks in her hand, squeezing hard enough to leave the red marks of her thumb on one cheek and four fingertips on the other, did not teach that child anything but to be afraid of or resentful of teachers' authority.

To learn is to integrate and live from the understanding you gain. You begin to live based on principles, even when you will neither be rewarded for nor avoid punishment with your actions. True learning is not likely to result from control.

If you're struggling with your reflection in this mirror, remember this: All of your interactions as a child wired your brain in a way that makes this kind of teaching seem comfortable for you. The great news for teachers is that we get to decide—to make a choice—about the kinds of connections we want to wire in children. Do we really want to make children automatons who only learn what is spoon-fed to them and who follow orders without question? Or do we want to wire brains that sustain children as lifelong learners, curious seekers, explorers, and inventors of the new?

I know I'm using an **I-Am-the-Boss-of-You** style with children, first and foremost, when I'm not really being my S.E.L.F. When I'm interacting with a child in a way that is not typical for how I interact with adults, I'm likely in this mode. A clear red flag is waved when I can't give children a good reason for what I'm asking them to do or not do. "Because I said so" is a clear signal of **The Boss** style.

Don't Feel Bad, Okay?

I'm hoping that, if you've read this far, you are getting my point about how we accidentally dim down children with this Anti-Sparkle Plan. By now, you've probably been thinking with sadness or guilt about some interactions you've had with children. I know I have. You may be feeling kind of bad about some of those interactions. I've been there.

Don't feel too badly for too long, okay? We have, each of us, at some time or other, likely dismissed or minimized the value of children in these ways. We all do it. To paraphrase Dr. Maya Angelou, we all do what we know until we know better; then we do better. So, feel a little bad, but just enough to make you want to keep reading and learn a different way.

Now let that bad feeling go. Set aside regrets. Don't beat yourself up. Now is the time for examining what you think you know and what you've been taught, which may not be working for most kids. Just look around you to remember how badly our status quo is working. Read the headlines.

Now is the time for learning a new way. Now is your time for knowing better. Tomorrow, you can do better.

The greatest cruelty of our relating to children as "cute," or from one of these places of patronizing, projecting, or bossing, is how it minimizes them as serious learners. Here's the most important lesson for ALL teachers to grasp: Children are learning ALL the time. From the moment they are born, they are learning. Every waking moment, they are learning. *There is nothing young children do that is NOT learning.* Always remember that.

So, if children are *always* watching and listening, they are *always* gathering key evidence to create their inner reality about who they are and how to interact with the world. By default, any nearby teacher is providing that example. All the time. Every second. That's why we need to be aware of the pedagogy—the method of teaching—embedded in our behavior. Every interpersonal interaction we have with a child, or in the presence of a child, is a lesson in social skills and emotional intelligence. We want to make sure the teaching practice of our own behavior delivers the understanding and skills we want to see in children.

Every teacher has a behavioral pedagogy, but they didn't learn it in school. This part of our teaching practice is where we act out all the now-subconscious meanings we crafted about relationships when we were young children. So, what's your behavioral pedagogy? The classroom environment includes the teacher as a key feature. You're teaching them something *about being a person* with how you behave, so what are you teaching them?

As you think about that, you may begin to realize just how intense the job of teacher really is. *Any* time a child can see or hear you, or feel your energetic impact, you are teaching them. No matter what you are doing, from talking to a parent, to filling out the federal food program paperwork, to explaining to a child the death of the classroom animal, to arguing with a co-teacher, to chatting with the principal in the doorway, in your best and worst moments, you are teaching all the children within eye- and earshot. *No matter what you are doing*, if there's a child around, they're learning something. Is it what you want them to learn?

In my experience, when this truth first dawns on teachers, many are at least a little horrified. You know how adults are. We're messy. We have unguarded moments, vulnerable moments, childish moments, tantrums, prissiness, and downright idiotic behavior. Sometimes our behavior is as bad as that for which we punish children.

When teachers realize that any child around them may observe, remember, and later imitate them or comment to others upon their less-than-stellar moments, they are likely to go into hiding. They don't literally dive into a hidey-hole. Yet most of us have adopted a role with children that hides who we really are. We pretend to be better than we really are for fear we aren't "good enough" as a model for children's learning.

I'm too messy to be a teacher! So I'm going to pretend to be perfect for the sake of being a better model for the children. I'm going to only show them strong and tough, never vulnerable or lost. I'm going to only show them hard work and faith, never exhaustion or self-doubt. Frankly, we adopt these roles in lots of relationships in our lives to prevent most people from seeing the whole glorious human mess we really are.

There is an alternative to all that, and it's why I wrote my first book. When we teachers focus so hard on being a Perfect Role Model for children, the result is that they never see the human condition in all its beauty and frailty. Worse, we are so busy adjusting our masks, we fail to see the children for who *they* are.

See Their Brilliance

I believe that our biggest error as teachers is that we assume a lack of capacity where there is enormous capacity—frankly, limitless capacity. We assume a void of *understanding* and completely miss the fascinating and instructive stories of *meaning* children are creating every moment. Then, when we hear them say something of astonishing insight, "cute" is the best feedback we can offer.

That, for me, is the crux of the matter. The brilliance of children has become like a fairy tale, and most teachers no longer believe in fairies. Perhaps fairies move at a speed so different from our own that we simply miss them? This is, I think, the way it works with children. So many teachers don't believe in the brilliance of children, so we miss it!

Then, without meaning to, we *dis*miss it. We act as if their communications, their opinions and feelings, and their understanding in a situation don't matter as much as ours. We act as if, since children can't yet speak our language, think rationally, don't know as much stuff, or have all our life experiences, they are somehow less valid as people than we are. We behave as if we believe that since they've taken in fewer data bytes of knowledge and experience, their output is not meaningful.

Here's another way to say it. We think that young children know and understand very little of the world. Therefore, what they say and do doesn't carry the importance that we tend to assume as the foundation of most adult expressions.

I believe we are wrong about that. *All of it.* Every child's behavior has meaning. Every. Single. Child. Every bit of their behavior. Every child's behavior is rich with communication. They are constantly expressing their understanding of the world, their inner reality.

What neuroscience has taught us is that human beings are meaning-making machines, starting from birth. In fact, each young child builds their own model of the world and the people in it as they simultaneously construct the architecture of their brains around that model. We humans literally design and build ourselves at the same time.

Adding to my most important message—that children are always learning, all the time—I also hope you remember the following: Whatever children do and say (1) is an expression of what they think, feel, and yearn for and, more importantly, (2) conveys the *meaning* they have created. Part one is pure Jean Piaget, one of the fathers of developmental psychology: everything children do and say is expressing their inner reality: thoughts, emotions, wishes, dreams, and—above all—*understanding*. Part two is brain development 101. Children's inner reality—the meaning they construct from the experiences they have—is wiring itself into their brains.

All children define themselves and the social world from this inner meaning. When we chuckle and label them "cute," or when we project our adult understanding onto them or focus on taming or controlling them, we dismiss that process and its amazing results.

Moving toward Teaching Sparkle Kids. Young children mostly need us to pay closer attention to them and take them more seriously. They need us to listen and to respond with the understanding that what they say and do, what they feel and yearn for, matters. It matters deeply. The rest of this book is about teaching from that point of view.

My fundamental advice for you is to take children as seriously as they take themselves. Teachers, then, have a dual-mindfulness challenge if we are to get beyond dismissing children's expressions of their meaningful inner world. The first is to slow down and pay attention—*real* attention—to what children are doing, saying, and feeling.

I believe each child is a unique gift that we must unwrap over time, finding all the layers of meaning there, learning how this child uniquely expresses in the world. We must constantly ask ourselves—or, better, find out through dialogue with the child—what does this behavior mean? What understanding is this child showing me? A very intuitive parent I once hired as a teacher assistant for a first-grade classroom put it very succinctly when she said, "I look behind the deed and see the need."

The second mindfulness challenge for teachers of young children is to consistently examine ourselves and increase the alignment of our own behavior—what we say and do—with the values we want to model for our children. The adages are all true: children learn much more about human community from watching what we do than from listening to what we tell them to do.

A child sculpts much of their interpretation of life—of "how things go"—from their observations of how adults seem to feel, what we seem to want, and how we interact with others in our world. If we're wearing masks over our human faces—not showing how we really feel and what we honestly think—then their learning is skewed in the direction of unreality. Also, our instructional lessons or authoritarian proclamations on how to behave are largely ignored in favor of deductive learning from their observations of our behavior. "Mind what I say, not what I do," just doesn't work!

Here's the worst news of all. "Monkey see, monkey do," is an excellent axiomatic summary of how young children learn by watching us. Unfortunately, it often seems to apply only to the very worst in us. Don't be fooled, though. Truly, children *also* see and imitate our kind, just, rational, loving, peaceful, thoughtful, authentic moments. However, when we are feeling the shame of watching their dramatic imitation of our must unattractive traits, it's hard to remember the last ten times we witnessed their imitation of our better self.

Something about looking in the mirror of a four-year-old child's caricature and seeing our most petty self reflected back can erase a mountain of other memories of our positive impact. Also unfortunate is the reality that, in those moments of seeing some part of our worst self in children, our own defensiveness often leads us to punish the child for imitating us. I have been an eyewitness to teachers scolding or putting children in time-out for the exact same behavior the teacher modeled earlier.

For teachers to adequately rise to this dual challenge of paying attention both to children's social and emotional integrity and to their own, the first requirement is to release "cute" as a single-word eraser of all that meaning children are making and expressing. Yes, children's behavior is sometimes endearing, a reminder of earlier innocence in ourselves. Yes, they make us say, "Awwww," sometimes involuntarily. That reaction is our innate programming as primates to find our young adorable. It's why they come with big eyes, and mouths shaped like hearts. They're supposed to be irresistible, and they are.

I don't want to beat this message drum too hard, but children desperately need for us to get past that *cute* response as our primary reaction. When you feel the *awwwww* rising, instead of proclaiming a child as *cuh-YOOT!*, try looking the child in the eyes and saying, "I feel so close/connected to you right now. I admire how you are in the world," and see what happens.

Cornerstone Strategies of the Seek Sparkle & Shine Plan

(aka Teaching to the Brilliance in a Young Child)

For the five styles of the Anti-Sparkle Plan, I offer five replacement cornerstones for teaching. The principles for the Seek Sparkle & Shine Plan also form a pentagon. This one creates a strong foundation under our kids rather than a fort from which to unintentionally wage war on their brilliance. My hashtags for these strategies are:

- #slowdowntunein – Slow Down, Tune In
- #seethemnotyou – See Them, Not You
- #thischildthismoment – This Child, This Moment
- #benewbebrave – Be New, Be Brave
- #staysanebeyourself – Stay Sane, Be Your S.E.L.F.

These five general strategies foster the age-specific Basic Tools for mining the *7 Childhood Treasures*. In the chapter on Treasure-Centered Teaching, I describe these Basic Tools along with some Broken Tools from the Anti-Sparkle Plan we can all stop using.

#slowdowntunein – Slow Down, Tune In

I once saw an episode of *Star Trek: Next Generation* in which a couple of characters shifted to another "phase." There, they moved at such an increased speed, compared to the rest of the crew, that their voices were like a mosquito whine in the ear, their passing like a whiff of breeze. This bit of science fiction captures perfectly the variance in speeds I see between the world of young children—especially newborns and toddlers—and the world of most adults.

Infants develop quickly and at a rapidly increasing rate from the moment of their first breath. Yet they can seem relatively unchanging, day by day, to those who care for them. We're often surprised when, suddenly, they seem "all grown up" from an earlier stage of development.

I'm often stunned by the sudden recognition that the once-floppy noodle of a newborn has firmed up. At about three months, a reorganization of a baby's central nervous system adds a little coherence to their body and intention to their movements. Then on a future day, the stumbling, inarticulate toddler seems to disappear, replaced by a fully interactive preschooler. In my personal Facebook feed, I often see the late-childhood, prepubescent children of my friends seemingly transformed overnight into young adults. The child is suddenly gone from their face and posture, and there is something newly grown-up in the directness of their gaze and the set of their shoulders.

Yet look at the infant's "sudden" maturation from the infant's perspective. Just in physical development alone, imagine the experience of transforming from a seven-pound, multi-limbed yet loose and fluid bundle, like a half-filled water balloon, with no large muscle control to a seventeen-pound center of gravity with fully articulated limbs and enough strength in your core muscles to sit upright without support. Then add all the development to coordinate reaching for and picking up objects. Then add all the social skills required to make your teacher laugh aloud! All that amazing capacity—and much, much more—emerges within 180 days.

Maybe you don't appreciate how much change that is. For example, before sitting up, you had to first develop enough musculature in your neck, chest, and upper back to hold that giant bowling ball of a head steady on top of your little baby body! That accomplishment alone took a few weeks. Over the first six months of your life, thousands of muscles matured, the vestibular system of the inner ear got turned on and asserted itself, your visual acuity sharpened, and your field of vision widened.

So many maturational changes occur to enable this miracle of sitting up and reaching for a toy without falling over. New capacities, including new neural connections, new strength and coordination in muscles, and soft bones becoming hard, were needed. If we catalogued every single facet of the growth that unfolds for this *one* capacity of sitting up unassisted, the average per-minute number of developmental events would astonish you.

Yet in the first 180 days of most children's developmental journey, these changes lined themselves up and unfolded, in just the right order, to reach this phenomenal end goal. If you think the accomplishment of sitting up and reaching for objects doesn't matter much, think about how little of your current life you could do without that ability.

A baby experiences every step forward, step backward, and pause in this multilayered physical change. They may reach for something dozens of times and fail to grasp it before the first success. They may topple over from a sitting position for weeks before they finally achieve balance. Simultaneously, they are experiencing other changes in their language, vision, social skills, and more. Truly, from the baby's perspective, these six months crawl by (pun completely intended) because *so much* is going on.

Now, for the infant teacher at the early learning center, these six months seem to zip by (even more so for the parents). With hundreds of diapers to change, feedings to manage, naps to rock into, onesies to change, in addition to the rest of the teacher's days—full of adult relationships, bills to pay, dogs to walk, their own children to rear—well, that time can go by in a blur.

Yes, we teachers feel that we've done a lot during those six months as they sped by, and yet, it is all like a passing mosquito whine to baby. Though their pace of awareness is slower, they have still managed to build a significant portion of their shiny, new neural network during that time, so maybe my workload was not as impressive as I thought.

Teachers race through busy, productive days. Meanwhile, the baby watching you from the saucer chair just ticked off a million new neural connections for items on their developmental to-do list in the time it took you to move the furniture for tummy time. Even though you're busy, you don't have to miss it all.

The first important strategy for early childhood teachers is simply to drop out of warp speed and tune into what the child in front of us is doing. Move the furniture but mindfully, aware of the child's participation. Talk with them about what you're doing.

Sometimes, just sit still. Simply watch them. Try it for fifteen minutes without distraction. Put someone else in charge of the group. It's okay to interact; if a child smiles at you, smile back. If they hand you something, take it and say, "thank you." Behave normally in response to the child's initiations, but initiate nothing yourself and don't take care of any of your business. Let the child take the lead, and you watch and follow when invited.

What do you see a child do during that fifteen minutes? Literally, can you make a specific, objective (that is, noninterpretive) list? Maybe the first sixty seconds would look like this for a three-month-old infant:

- Lying on tummy, supporting head and upper torso on forearms
- Pushes right hand along blanket toward toy giraffe; bumps into it and pushes it farther away
- Pulls arm back and drags the blanket too; giraffe is pulled closer

Cornerstone Strategies of the Seek Sparkle & Shine Plan

- Eyes widen, mouth opens, makes a "huh" sound and laughs a little
- Releases blanket, picks up right hand, reaches and grabs giraffe's front legs
- Eyes widen, mouth opens, makes a "huh" sound and drops giraffe
- Looks up at me, frowns and makes fussy noises; I smile and say, "Try again"
- Fusses at me a little more; I smile and wait, and they look back at giraffe after a few seconds
- Picks up right hand, reaches, and grabs giraffe's neck and head
- Makes a "huh" sound and laughs a little; waves the giraffe a bit and looks up at me, smiling

Now, imagine watching a baby at this level of detailed attention for the whole fifteen minutes—fourteen more minutes of the above. How much might you learn about a child's actual capacities—for movement, response to patterns, communication, and social connection—if you watched for fifteen minutes out of every two hours whenever the child is awake?

The level of freedom to observe this often may not be possible in your learning environment. Even without this kind of luxury for observation, here's your motivator to slow down as much as you can: All child behavior communicates the child's current understanding of self, world, expectations, sense of safety, willingness to risk, and so much more. Think of the authentic connection you can create with this child simply by slowing down enough to receive all those rich signals.

Great early-years teachers know that a significant key to understanding a child's current developmental status is observation—not just once, but repeated observations over time. One example of a behavior is something to notice and wonder about. Seeing the same behavior twice makes it more interesting. Then, at three times, we may begin to form a hypothesis about what the child understands.

Teachers who #slowdowntunein strive to see these emerging patterns well enough to "scaffold" a child's next experience, to create an accessible step-up to the next understanding. They begin by hypothesizing a child's current understanding, doing their best to decode the child's behavior. Then they offer an experience to expand on that understanding.

To see all there is to see, we need to put our adult mind and life in neutral sometimes. That's strategy number one in the Seek Sparkle & Shine Plan: #slowdowntunein.

#seethemnotyou – See Them, Not You

Strategy number two is to really see the child in front of you rather than projecting yourself onto the child. It's more of a challenge than you might think! Truly seeing a child—or any other person, for that matter—requires a commitment to curiosity rather than evaluation. Yet we are a culture structured around evaluation of others. Each of us consumed the inclination toward evaluative judgment from birth, as if blended into the milk we drank and the food we ate. If you disagree, bear with me here, and I'll demonstrate.

First, let me say that evaluative judgment isn't necessarily negative. We judge attributes positively too, and on some rare occasions, we stay neutral. Still, whenever I "decide" what someone else is "like," I'm evaluating and judging them. Even if my judgment is that the person is kind and considerate, it's still my judgment. I am the one who made meaning out of a set of variables and then named it.

Learning from early childhood to judge and label is now our culture's default. By the time we're adults, we are inclined to judge even babies.

We begin before they're born, attributing expectations for temperament, appearance, and capacities. All these judgments may be solely based on the gender announced at a reveal party. Then, from birth, we label them for their impact on us rather than trying to understand their experience. That may be difficult to see at first. From which of the two columns below do you hear more comments from teachers about infants and toddlers?

Seeing Self	Seeing Them
Baby is a poor napper. It takes forever to get him back to sleep whenever he wakes.	Baby is learning to self-soothe and napped poorly today. He seems overtired right now.
I can't keep the classroom floor clean with these messy kids throwing everything off the trays.	They're learning about cause and effect and gravity via the high-chair trays these days.
He's so defiant! He must learn to mind me, to do what I say, but he's getting sneakier now.	He's really discovering what he wants now. My vigilance has to be higher now; he's so fearless!
She's such a little bully, always taking toys away from the other children her age and younger.	She's not yet able to share well, so we're helping her see her impact on other people's feelings.

Even when they've dumped the spices out of their sensory jars and added liquid glue to finger paint on the floor, can you enter this experience from the child's point of view rather than your own? Imagining the sensory stimulation and rich learning of that experience for them, rather than going straight to anger over the mess to clean up, is one sign that you've mastered this strategy from the Seek Sparkle & Shine Plan.

Remember that several styles in the Anti-Sparkle Plan involve projecting the teacher's meaning for behavior or emotional state onto the behavior of a child. This second strategy invites you to strengthen your own boundaries—the edges that separate you from the child who is here before you: a unique, special gift to the world, as *you* are. You can #seethemnotyou.

#thischildthismoment – This Child, This Moment

Speaking of the unique, special gift to the world that is each child, unique does mean *unique*—one of a kind, no one else like them. Each one-of-a-kind child is growing in their own time, at their own pace, along their own path. Though there are general trends that make us human beings all similar in significant ways, we are also each a singularity.

We share a common humanity, yet each of us maps an individualized set of experiences onto that shared developmental framework. Groups of us share a common culture, shaped for each of us by the ways in which the environment has affected our growing up. Environmental factors, such as our food and nutrition, the play and learning materials we have access to, and other humans' interactions with us, all matter.

Even within one family, where two or more children are raised by the same adults, the experience of each child is unique. Naive, first-time parents can become wiser before their youngest children come along many years later. Times change, too, and influences change with them. For example, the teen music of the thirteen-year-old eldest sibling in 1983 (The Police, Styx, Eurythmics, David Bowie, Journey, and *Flashdance*) carried different messages of social and political influence than the music of the youngest sibling, who turned thirteen in 1988 (Bobby McFerrin, Phil Collins, Bon Jovi, U2, Tracy Chapman).

Within a classroom of children who all turned five years old during the same twelve-month span, each one is at a unique intersection of maturation and experience. Each one certainly comes from a different family background. In many early learning settings not tied to neighborhood-based schools, children often come from different neighborhoods and different cultures. A teacher cannot teach one way for twenty-five kindergartners; they must often teach twenty-five ways, or at least a dozen or so!

Similar to the #seethemnotyou strategy, #thischildthismoment asks you to be aware of a unique person at a unique moment in time. This strategy, though, widens the #seethemnotyou view, asking you to go beyond how this child is not you to clarify how this child is not anyone else. After this necessary first step, #thischildthismoment also asks you to be aware of this unique moment in this child's lifelong developmental journey.

It seems only common sense when you hear it like this: We cannot expect the same capacity in a child of six months as we find in a child of sixteen months. By logical extension, we cannot expect the same capacity in a child of forty-eight months (four years) as we find in a child of forty-eight months and one month…or even one day.

In fact, because of the nature of child development, which flows forward and back like a series of irregular coastal tides, a child's capacity at 6:00 A.M. may be quite different from the one observed at 10:30 A.M. The child who clearly understands something new on Tuesday can show total confusion about the same topic on Wednesday. Especially when children are on a cusp, living in the midst of the disequilibrium that drives them from one stage or phase of development to another, these swings in capacity can be wide and rapidly moving.

Just as importantly, we should not expect that a seven-year-old understands the world as their five-year-old self did. When we lock children into labels too young, we sometimes take away their right and ability to grow beyond that label. As long as we keep expecting it and labeling it, we will keep seeing it. What if we stopped expecting it? What if we shifted to more asking, more seeking to understand, rather than labeling?

Children's developmental processes reveal that teaching is most effective, and best reaches children's brilliance, when we are authentically with this child, in this moment. When we are responsive to the current truth, the current reality, the current capacity of this specific child, we lift that child further in a moment than if we used, for a whole year, only those strategies targeted to the median/average/norm expected for the age group. That is the essence of the #thischildthismoment strategy.

#benewbebrave – Be New, Be Brave

To introduce the fourth strategy, I offer a quote from Kahlil Gibran, the Lebanese-American poet and author of *The Prophet*. In his poem "On Children," he addressed these words to parents: "You can strive to be like [children], but seek not to make them like you. For life goes not backward nor tarries with yesterday." To teach children in preparation for their lives of the future requires that we release our attachment to our pasts. We must make ourselves "new."

Of course, we do influence children from our history of experience; the past has some value. Yet children do not, and never will, need to learn to be like us in every way, especially in the sense of how they cope with their lives. You know why? Their lives are radically different from ours. Yes, some values and success strategies are timeless and do translate from one generation to another. Many, many other lessons you have learned and your tidbits of advice from your life experiences are usually as relevant to the lives of the youngest generation as a bicycle is to a fish.

My mother grew up without television, a central factor that shaped the zeitgeist of my generation. Then I grew up without computers or cell phones, a central factor shaping the generations that follow mine. The earliest arrivals in my Baby Boomer generation grew up learning to hide under their desks as protection from nuclear bombs. Their great-grandchildren's generation, growing up now, learns the same behavior as protection from automatic gunfire.

Indeed, except for occasional retro trends in art, design, and fashion, "life goes not backward." Life evolves; it is ever-changing. Clothing, music, and behavior that are scandalous in one generation of teenagers will often seem a model of modesty and decorum when compared to the scandals of their children, once they reach the magical age of teen rebellion. As I recall her story, my mother's poodle skirt in the 1940s sent my grandmother into a fit as dramatic as the one Mom had over miniskirts in the 1960s.

When we pretend that their childhoods are echoes of our own, we accidentally dismiss children's experiences. When we create strategies for children in either blind imitation or reactive rejection of our parents' and teachers' strategies, we dismiss their current realities. When we remain ignorant of current social and political forces that affect children, we are asking them for bravery beyond our own.

Assuming children are living some repetition of our youth invades our connection with them. When we reject the latest research knowledge about children and what they need, relying on "wisdom" handed down by our parents and teachers, we say to children, "Your current reality doesn't matter as much as my memories."

"Now, let me tell you how much easier you have it than I did at your age…" It's a classic joke that adults exaggerate the arduous realities of their youth—walking five miles to school, uphill both directions in blizzards, for example—and it's funny because it's true. It's true that we adults exaggerate, but it's also true that our lives were radically different from those being lived by the children of today.

When we teachers "keep up" with the ever-changing world by striving to be more "like" the children, as Gibran suggested, we benefit almost as much as they do. Of course, being like them is not about being childish or immature. It is about being connected to what the kids are connected to. It is watching their TV, listening to their music, and—most of all—listening to *them*. Just as we observe greater detail when we #slowdowntunein, we can understand children's world better by being brave enough to hear about it directly from them.

That act takes great courage. You must be a super brave teacher to face the world that children face rather than the gentler one you imagine for them. Truly, their world is more terrifying than the one we live in. Young children, especially before the "age of reason" emerges around six years, simply cannot see the same world we see. Without the benefits of logic to aid their understanding, the world can seem either glittering and magical or dark and sinister.

Try putting yourself into a child's life, imitating as best you can what it is like for them. At least, try to adopt the physical experience. Get down on your knees and look around at the world. See how much bigger than you everything is, including people. Lie on your back, pretending you are unable to make purposeful movements with your arms and legs. Can you imagine, for just one second, what it would be like to suddenly have some huge being, four or five times your size, swoop in and abruptly lift you into the air? Can you feel in your body how terrifying that would be? Imagine some giant suddenly picking you up right now.

Can you imagine, or pretend to imagine, what it's like to confront a barking dog whose snarling teeth are right at the height of your head? Or see a giant, angry teacher come striding toward you with a human snarl on their face? Probably you will fall short of how scary those experiences can be for a young one, but it's worth the effort to imagine it. Maybe just imagine the mundane experience of living in a world in which all the doorknobs are out of reach. Even if you can't fully sympathize with children's experiences—really sharing that emotion or physical sensation—you'll at least be more empathetic for your efforts.

Again, children do not need you to be perfect at this strategy on the first day you use it. You do not need to completely understand a child's experience of the world and how it differs from yours. Your courage to "be new" is your willingness to admit you don't know. Your bravery is in the striving to know. There it is, the fourth strategy: #benewbebrave. There is just one more point to place in this five-cornered foundation.

#staysanebeyourself – Stay Sane, Be Your S.E.L.F.

This last cornerstone strategy in the Seek Sparkle & Shine Plan creates both your touchstone (to stay "sane") and your need to continue growing. First, teachers all need to stay sane when we're "in charge" of children. I'm of the strong opinion that the kids are Job One for us during the hours when we are "on duty."

When children are awake, I'm on deck if I'm the teacher. Period. Other responsibilities and interests take a back seat to the child's interests as I stay poised for one of those fabulous "teachable moments."

When a child's readiness and curiosity hold wide the doors to a new level of understanding, I'm 100 percent focused in the moment, with all these five cornerstone strategies beneath my feet. To stay slowed down, tuned in, focused on this child, in this moment, and all the rest—to stay what I think of as "sane" with children—requires me to live in a Little

Red House well anchored by the *7 Childhood Treasures*. It requires that I drive my C.A.R. into that relationship with the child.

Say what?

My first book, *Just Be Your S.E.L.F.—Your Guide to Improving Any Relationship*, describes how adults can mine the *7 Childhood Treasures* for themselves with Development Do-Overs. My observation has been that many of us left early childhood without these assets, and we can't support the mining work of children unless we have completed our own efforts. There's a whole section coming up next to clarify these terms and how they work together.

What follows is a summary of highlights from that first book to give us some shared language for the rest of this book-length journey together. If you've already read *Just Be Your S.E.L.F.*, you can skip or skim this material. If you haven't, then I strongly encourage you to go beyond this summary. Read my first book and work through the Development Do-Overs it contains. When you better understand the strengths I'm encouraging you to foster in children through the cornerstone strategies, you will find more success with these strategies.

So, that introduces the S.E.L.F. half of this strategy. Supporting children with tools as they mine the Treasures for themselves requires you to be an experienced miner yourself. Have you looked at your own history of access to these Childhood Treasures like Trust, Independence, Negotiation, and Acceptance? Did you mine them all and build a Little Red House as a safe home for your personality? Are you showing up for your relationships full of Choice, Agency, and Responsibility? The explanations of these concepts in the next chapter will help you answer these questions.

My strongest opinion about early education may be that the children need you to make this effort for them. You will only be your Self-governed, Ego-aware, Leading, Free self—your S.E.L.F.—when you possess these seven precious assets. Without ensuring the healthy status of *your* Treasures, your best efforts to implement the strategies in this book may show few results. Indeed, you may unwittingly be keeping kids out of their mine shafts and away from their Treasures.

Without doing your own mining work first, you may just be one more blind adult leading another generation of children into your darkness.

The "Short Course"

Until you read *Just Be Your S.E.L.F* **in full…**

Children need more adults in their lives who understand at least the basics of their developmental pathways for social and emotional development. If you're ready to be one of those teachers who understand this elegant and universal pattern for early social and emotional development, then this little summary will give you the basics.

The essential point of my first book is that each of us succeeds in life chiefly through relationships with others. Both at home and at work, we are happy in our relationships only to the extent that we mined, cut, and polished *7 Childhood Treasures* between birth and seven years of age. If you want kids to sparkle, to shine, to succeed, they need these seven relationship assets. They can't find them without your help, and you can't help them unless you've found yours!

The younger the better for that mining work, but it's not too late for older children. In fact, *Just Be Your S.E.L.F.* reveals how adults can retrace the developmental pathways of those crucial early years now. Yes, adults and older children, with help, can redo the mining job. It's never too late to uncover these seven capacities crucial to joyful, productive lives.

Your Little Red House and C.A.R.

I created the story of a home base for your personality called the Little Red House as a way to remember the Treasures and how they work together. Here's one image, and you may envision a different sort of house. Regardless of what you see in your mind's eye, know that this two-dimensional safe home—a square with a triangle on top—is anchored at its seven key junctions with these Treasures: the capacities for Trust, Independence, Faith, Negotiation, Vision, Compromise, and Acceptance.

- Trust and Independence anchor the two sides of your foundation as the bottom of the square.
- Faith relies on Trust as its base, so it holds up the top of the square on one side of the foundation.
- Negotiation cannot be successful without Independence, so it holds the top of the square on that side of the foundation.
- Vision balances on top of Trust and Faith, holding up one roof eave, a bottom corner of the triangle.
- Compromise balances on top of Independence and Negotiation, holding up the other roof eave as the other bottom corner of the triangle.
- Acceptance is impossible without the other six Treasures and protects them all, as the roof peak, the top corner of the triangle.

Life in a stable, sturdy, well-anchored Little Red House enables you to manufacture the high-test, three-part fuel you need to drive your Choice-Agency-Responsibility mobile. When you leave the secure home base of your Little Red House for adventures in relationships with other humans, you travel in your C.A.R.

Individuation: A Life Journey

Another key message of *Just Be Your S.E.L.F.* is that the life of a child is one long process of individuation. They separate from the influential adults in their life as models for how to be *them*. With each developmental stage, children find new ways of saying, "I am me. I am NOT you!" to their parents, teachers, and other significant adults.

Yet the journey of individuation is not a direct straight line outward, moving ever farther away from the point of origin. This developmental "pathway" is more of a pulsing out and back, out and back. It begins when an infant first crawls a few feet away then hustles back to home base. Later, children move away from the home-base security of a neighborhood school, even a city of birth, and eventually, the family home. Yet they still "return" now and then for a safety check, later moving outward again, a little farther the next time, and a little farther the time after that.

This extended individuation integrates three growth processes that interact: Maturation, Teaching and Learning, and Construction. These three strands of developmental processes braid together and, over time, create the adult human.

Maturation is, as it sounds, simply growing up. This process runs on the predictor hardware in all our systems. If development is on track, certain milestones show up at expected ages. Our bodies grow taller, stronger, and better coordinated; our ability to understand language emerges on a timetable; we all begin to be logical by about age six. As surely as the sun will rise, maturational development occurs, on its own, without any need to encourage it.

Teaching and Learning is the developmental process by which we acquire conventional knowledge from some other person or resource. Conventional knowledge is whatever we cannot mature into or "figure out" unless someone tells us; it begins with the names of things, such as letters, numbers, and shapes. You cannot mature enough to know or figure out by yourself that this shape ○ is called "circle," if English is the language you're learning. Someone tells you this name, and when you name it correctly in the future, you are rewarded by a treasured adult's response of, "That's right! It's a circle!"

Construction is the juiciest and most fascinating aspect of our development. We each literally build certain aspects of our knowledge. Especially important to this book is that each of us constructs our own understanding of the social world. We come to understand who we are, what our value is, who others are (by groups and as individuals), and *their* value, all through a construction process. We build what we know. The people in our world—particularly the parents and teachers—provided us all the tools for this job.

The 7 Childhood Treasures

When teachers provide the right tools at the right time, children are able to mine these seven valuable social assets between birth and seven years of age:

Trust – The willingness to be dependent, believing that your needs will be met by others. We have Trust when we can be less powerful than another without fear.

Independence – Taking leadership in your life with compassion and understanding, and without isolation. The ability to discern what is you and yours from what is not. The capacity to feel both your personal edges and your interpersonal connections.

Faith – The capacity to believe in something impossible, a Big Dream that is larger than you and your life. The ability to let your mind soar beyond known limits.

Negotiation – The skill of managing how limits and agreements shape your relationships. Learning where your boundaries—your mental, emotional, and psychological "skins"—press against others', and how to make choices "inside the box" of their limits.

Vision – The allowing of Big Ideas; the capacity to invent, create, play, and pretend. The ability to make plans and bring them to fruition. Learning to see and reach for what is "outside the box."

Compromise – The ability and willingness to find resolution, common ground, shared understanding. The capacity to work toward the places of intersection.

Acceptance – The capacity to engage with life's diversity rather than being passively affected or victimized by it. The ability to cope with the reality that sometimes there is no compromise, that "bad things" happen to good people.

These *7 Childhood Treasures*, then, serve as the anchor bolts to connect all the corners and joints in your Little Red House. They are what make your safe home of personality a sturdy structure that can protect you from life's storms.

But, teacher, you will be unable to foster their mining of these Treasures by the children you teach if you cannot:

- Believe your needs can be met by others.
- Allow yourself to be vulnerable to others.
- Assume leadership in your own life rather than being its passive victim.
- Demonstrate compassion and understanding for yourself and others.
- Feel connected rather than isolated.
- Believe in yourself and your dreams.
- Develop successful win-win solutions when conflict arises.
- Live a life of invention, a life that expresses your innate creativity.

- Joyfully find the intersections between your unique self and diverse others.
- Establish yourself as an agent—an initiator—in your own life.

If this life doesn't sound like yours, then I again strongly recommend my first book, *Just Be Your S.E.L.F.—Your Guide to Improving Any Relationship*. My Development Do-Overs absolutely work, and the book is full of them—activities you do in the workbook-style pages if you have a soft-cover copy. Or download the e-book and re-create those exercises with paper and pen. Your choice! You *can* live the life described above if you want it. I encourage you to get the book and start digging for your seven gems!

Treasure-Centered Teaching

Early childhood teachers partner with parents to support the development of a competent adult, almost from day one. There is no stage of development during which these teachers can "coast," take it easy, or otherwise relax on the job. Every moment with the child matters. Every. Moment. Matters.

It's a little terrifying, isn't it? Well, good news: children don't need us to be perfect. A Sparkle Kid grows in an environment that is *mostly* responsive to the stage-by-stage drivers of their Maturation and Construction, without requiring 100 percent perfect responsiveness. To be a *good enough* teacher is enough. Don't get me wrong. *Good enough* is still a big challenge for most of us.

My extended use of the metaphor for mining the **7 Childhood Treasures** from the earth is going to be a lot of fun now. In essence, I cast you, teacher, as the keeper of the company toolshed for our little miners. From your ropes, pickaxes, hammers, and grinders—your strategies and Basic Tools for Teaching and Learning—they receive what they need for mining the Treasures.

First, we must stop handing children the Broken Tools of the Anti-Sparkle Plan or asking them to dig with their bare hands. You can see how that would not go well. Often, they get a glimpse of, but don't get to mine, the Treasures. Some children never see the opening to the mine shaft at all.

Here's what you can expect of my teaching in the rest of the book. First, I'll link each Treasure to a driving force of Maturation and a driving force for Construction. We start with what is emerging naturally—maturing—within the child. Then we add how the child is currently creating understanding—constructing it. From the intersection of these two, it will be easy to discern which Cornerstone Strategies and tools are the right ones to employ in the Teaching and Learning aspect of development, in which you play a significant role. I conclude the section on each Childhood Treasure by describing some Broken Tools from the Anti-Sparkle Plan and suggesting some Basic Tools from the Seek Sparkle & Shine Plan.

The Dynamics of Mining Trust

One of a small number of highly significant Maturation drivers for the first nine to fifteen months of life is mastery of physical coordination. A baby's

> **TRUST**
> Maturation driver—Physical independence
> Construction driver—Will my needs be met?

innate program for the first year includes the transformation from a floppy noodle to an upright, walking biped. Born utterly dependent on outside caregiving, children become a great deal less dependent in one year as they individuate through motor development.

The Construction process of children's development during this same period is driven by the question of whether their needs will be met. They want to know whether somebody "has their back." A newborn's complete and utter physical dependence on adults is the perfect setup to invoke the need for trust. Newborns cannot fulfill even their most basic needs for survival. They *must* rely on us and then learn whether we will come through for them. The most intense period for this construction of Trust is the period of greatest dependence, between birth and six months.

To become Sparkle Kids, infants need teachers whose Teaching and Learning focus is almost entirely on meeting their needs. Your Cornerstone Strategies of #slowdowntunein and #seethemnotyou are essential in these earliest weeks of life.

No need for flash cards or classical music to create a superbaby. Their natural brilliance shines already. You just need to slow down enough to see it. Then take it a step further to *really* see it, without your projections or interpretations.

As the infant becomes more independent—holding up their head, "scooching," sitting up, crawling, pulling up to standing, walking—and their needs continue to be met most of the time, that raw ore of Trust pulled up in the first six months is cut to reveal its beautiful facets. As needs continue to be met, the gem of Trust is polished to a high sheen, sparkling and ready to go into the foundation of this infant's Little Red House!

As a baby transitions into a toddler, with the advent of walking independently, our Teaching and Learning focus expands to helping them learn to meet some of their own needs. Older babies can learn how to soothe their minor upsets, for example, put themselves to sleep, and persevere through minor frustration. Yes, all this is—or can be—in a baby's repertoire *well* before one year of age.

For your Teaching and Learning tools, you'll want to ditch some old broken familiars in favor of some shiny new Basic Tools for Treasure mining.

Broken Tools

Let Them Cry. Sooner or later, someone will tell you, "You spoil infants if you always pick them up when they cry or carry them around too much." No, you cannot. Let me repeat that: you CANNOT spoil an infant. Infants cannot be spoiled, if what you mean is that they will become ruined little beings who cannot get along with others.

This old-fashioned Broken Tool rises from the Wild Child Tamer archetype of the Anti-Sparkle Plan. It also dates from a time before we saw the neural scans of infants, showing the reality inside the brain. When a newborn baby cries and nobody comes to find out what's wrong, their brain wires up some neurons from that experience. Let's suppose they are cold or hungry, in pain or uncomfortable, or perhaps just awake and alone. For an infant, who doesn't know yet that people they can't see continue to exist, being alone must be terrifying.

From whichever of these needs is felt, the baby communicates first with a bit of a fuss and rustle. It's as if you turned to your spouse and said calmly, "Could you come here, please? I need you." Then baby gets louder and more active in their calling out for help. You'd be adding a little urgency to your voice and raising your volume a bit to be sure you're heard: "Honey! Did you hear me? I need you!" The longer they wait for a relieving response, the more baby's expressions of discomfort grow in volume and energy, just as yours do. At the point at which an infant breaks into a full-throated cry for help, you would be yelling at your spouse and using every curse word you usually don't to tell them to get themselves over to you RIGHT NOW BECAUSE IT'S URGENT, YOU #@!%*@ IDIOT!!

Eventually, if the scenario of "nobody comes when I cry out from my need" repeats again and again, those neurons that first fired together on the first occurrence now gather more neurons to join their little understanding of the world. More and more connections are made around the experience of "nobody comes."

This network grows, with each experience of crying out in vain for help becoming an ever-expanding cluster of interconnected neurons. The neurons fire together—zap-zippety-ZAP!—over and over, building a stronger network of understanding about how life is: Nobody comes. This bleak and lonely understanding of the first human relationships forms the foundation for how and who we trust later in life.

Now, imagine the neural network that is built when somebody *does* come help when the baby cries in need. A soft voice murmurs soothingly as gentle hands cradle and lift the whimpering baby. Their whole body, from tucked knees to cheek, is pulled into warm and humming contact with the body of the adult who has come to relieve the distress. The cold, the wet, and clammy, the pain in the middle—whatever the distress is—it is relieved and replaced with better conditions: warm, dry, full, and sleepy.

See the different neurons connecting, firing, and strengthening to store and then build upon this fundamental definition of relationships, this understanding of "how life is"? Which neural network do you want to build?

Learning Starts Later. Once, a staff member at the agency where I worked asked a roomful of early education teachers the age at which learning begins. The vast majority chose age five or six. That's a shocking outcome in this population. Yet I am confounded by this belief from the Patronizing Passerby playbook all too often, especially among teachers of the very young. "Babies are no more than a sack of potatoes; they're not really learning anything."

The fact is that 85 percent of a child's brain is built between birth and three years of age. Three! You may have heard that 95 percent of the brain is constructed by age five, and that is true. But did you know that it's at 85 percent by age three? Certainly, there is plenty of learning going on from the moment of birth to make that happen. Even if you're not intentional in what you teach, you're still teaching *something.*

Basic Tools

The best strategy for babies from the Seek Sparkle & Shine Plan is *#slowdowntunein*. To notice the sometimes-subtle cues a nonverbal baby gives you about what they are learning, doing, and needing requires focus. Fortunately, that's not too painful a task as babies are fascinating!

At first, they need us to understand signals and cues for their "need of the moment." Typically, those early needs are simple, and the cues that signal them are obvious. This cry is for hunger, that one for a wet tushy, these red eyes and irritable noises mean sleepy, that gurgling coo means time for play.

As they get older and more mobile, babies' needs get more complex and so do their communications. Our job is to be present, respond, and then course-correct our action if what we've done doesn't seem to meet the need. Three Basic Tools address the "be present and respond" parts of the job.

Respond…Even to Silence. Young infants need feeding, changing, and rocking. They need to interact and play, rest and sleep. They need relief from discomfort and opportunities to explore and learn in a safe world. No matter which of these needs is primary at the moment, the pattern for mining Trust is the same. The infant needs, and an infant teacher meets the need.

Pick them up when they cry; comfort them. Feed them when they're hungry; change them when they're wet or soiled. When their eyes lock on yours, stay connected and smile. Give them time "alone" on their tummies with some interesting toys to look at and reach for while you quietly watch nearby.

When you're changing diapers, prepping bottles, packing for a stroller walk, or other mundane activities, and babies are watching you, talk to them! Respond to their silent observation, which is a form of communication. Infants are endlessly fascinated by what you're doing, so give them the words for it as you do it.

Talk about what they're doing, too, and about what's happening in the world around you. As much as you can, describe everything they see and hear rather than what you're doing. The difference is subtle but important. Yes, it will sound silly at first to narrate activity. Give eye contact and use voice inflection as if in a real conversation with baby. Pretty soon, you will be.

Over time, teachers and babies create routines of care, a series of choreographed dances. When these dances repeat a few hundred times over the first two months of life, Trust is mined. At the same time, babies begin to adopt and adapt. They begin learning to meet their own needs, such as switching from rubbing a teacher's finger on sore gums to rubbing a teething toy when teacher is not near.

Mirror. When teachers imitate the vocal sounds, facial expressions, and movements of infants, they are mirroring. This pattern matching builds the connection between adult and child and supports the mining of the Treasure of Trust.

Most of us naturally behave this way; we're genetically programmed to respond to infants as a strategy for survival of the species. We are often not fully conscious of what we're doing, so good teachers become more so. Great teachers become not only conscious of, but intentional and planful in their mirroring.

#seethemnotyou and #thischildthismoment are the strategies that lead to greatness for infant teachers. The more you can be a simple mimic—adding nothing of your own but being a true mirror of the child's movements—the more influential your mirroring. Can you monkey-see, monkey-do without making changes that add your personality or make you look better? This child, in this moment, may be blowing you a raspberry—that wet spray of vibrating tongue between lips. If you repeat it back, in the same way, that's being a mirror.

Return the Serve. As infants get older, these kinds of predictable patterns begin to invite a more complex interaction tango. When babies begin to use sounds, gestures, and facial expressions to connect, they sound exactly like an adult speaking in full sentences, with one exception. In their "speech," random sounds replace known words. Pauses, changes in tone, the rising inflection for questions—it's all there in this early nonword speech we call babbling. This early speech also is rich with nonverbals: pointing and reaching, picking up and examining, focusing their eyes and attention.

Our job as teachers is to respond to these initiations as if in an actual conversation: with eye contact, words, facial expressions, and other actions that are appropriate to the context of the baby's communication. This "serve-and-return" dialogue with older infants and young toddlers creates strong neural connections in the communications and social skills regions of the brain.

Serve and return is like any game where a ball goes back and forth between two players or two teams. It looks fun because it is! One charming example of this kind of conversation can be found in some videos of the comedian DJ Pryor and his young toddler son, Kingston. I found them online easily in the summer of 2019, and I suspect they'll always be available on search. A great professional resource is an excellent how-to video by the Center on the Developing Child at Harvard University, which could be found online in late 2019 at https://developingchild.harvard.edu/science/key-concepts/serve-and-return/. This six-minute video includes many examples of day-to-day interactions between adults and children to illustrate the specifics of returning the serve.

In addition to #slowdowntunein and seethemnotyou, this Basic Tool for mining the Treasure of Trust uses the #thischildthismoment strategy. Each serve-and-return conversation is a unique learning moment for a unique child. Yet they all wire the brain into one pattern of trust: I initiate, and others see and hear my interest and respond.

These three Basic Tools give infants a great start in mining their raw ore of Trust. These kinds of interactions tell them the world has their back, and someone is there for them. This age is when children learn the powerful lesson, "I am not alone." Sadly, too many learn the opposite lesson.

Discovering the Boundaries of Independence

The driver of Maturation in the toddler is autonomy—self-governance—with which they take a giant leap into individuation. The old-fashioned word "sovereignty" sums

> **INDEPENDENCE**
>
> Maturation driver—Autonomy
> Construction driver—What is me/not me?

up a toddler's maturational force nicely, but nobody uses that word anymore, so autonomy and self-governance will do as mostly accurate synonyms.

A new interpersonal day is dawning for toddlers as they begin to discover where they "end" and the rest of the world "begins." I mean that quite literally. Self-awareness of the physical boundary that is the edge of their body begins to develop between three and six months of age, and awareness gradually unfolds that there are other boundaries.

Therefore, a pattern of a teacher consistently responding to an infant's needs in those first six months provides baby with the gift and curse of this consciousness: I am a separate self, an individual. Without the language or cognition to name it or think about it, a child begins to show they understand in a holistic sensory construction that Piaget called a *schema*. One day, you suddenly see that they understand: there is a "me" who needs something and an "other" who comes to meet that need. Maturation paired with our Teaching and Learning of showing up enable the infant to develop what Piaget called Object Permanence. They now know that we continue to exist when out of their sight.

Thus, the physical boundary of our skin comes into awareness. Baby learns that "I'm ME, here inside my skin, and I need something." And "You, teacher, are YOU, somewhere else inside your skin, even when I can't see you, and you provide what is needed." Object permanence pulls open the mine shaft to reveal the raw ore of Trust. Adults' continued responsiveness helps the mini miner get to digging and setting Trust into the foundation of the Little Red House. With the help of a great infant teacher, this child has begun to build a safe home for their personality.

The older infant's and then the toddler's growing motor and verbal skills confirm and begin to expand this basic new awareness of a self separate from others. The first time an older baby crawls away from the home base of a teacher's lap and then looks back at the gap between them, there is a look of surprise—almost shock—a little frisson of fear stirred into joyful surprise. Well, that look is priceless!

At first, separating from us—individuating from us—is only at this "entry level" of the physical (e.g., my body is hungry; your body brings the food). Later, boundaries come to include the understanding that we are separate from others mentally, emotionally, and energetically. In fact, this growing awareness is at the heart of the massive betrayal that is toddlerhood.

I know you cannot remember, but can you imagine knowing with absolute certainty that someone else shares your every thought, emotion, and whim of a desire? Can you conjure up the sense of security you'd feel if you were certain that you were completely understood, without effort, by your protectors and loved ones? Oh, the bliss of never doubting that your emotional state is completely shared and comprehended! Imagine how it felt to know that you would get whatever you wanted because someone out there wants it *for you* as intensely as you want it for yourself. What a great world, eh?

Now, take a breath…imagine the betrayal of finding out none of that is true. Sorry, you are not understood perfectly without any effort at communication. Your protectors have emotions that are different from yours, and they don't always know what yours are. Sometimes, your protector even refuses you the thing you most want, on the bizarre grounds that you *should not want it*! Other times, people take away the things you want because they want them for themselves. Shocking!

Seriously, do you know what it's like to have the world turned upside down on you in a moment? To suddenly learn that everything you thought you knew is flat wrong? It's horrifying, I promise you.

My past experience with groups of teachers tells me that some of you are receiving a little shock at this moment. First, let me confirm what you are hearing: nobody accurately knows what anyone else thinks and feels unless there is some curiosity and a conversation to find out. The widespread notion that we can know what someone else thinks or feels because we witness a fleeting expression or fail to get a prompt response is simply false. The internal world of your feelings, thoughts, and interests is likely what you are focused on most of the time, as I am focused on my internal world most of the time. My response to you is much more likely about what's going on inside me than it is about you. My sincere apologies for the jolt if that's news to you. Because I didn't have any boundaries until I was more than 35-years old, I remember my awakening to this reality, and it was painful.

This betrayal, I believe, is the source of the toddler's Construction driver to understand "what is me" and "what is not me." Therefore, they are passionate to express and receive recognition for the independent thinker within themselves. They crave your acknowledgment of the fiercely felt emotions in their little bodies and need you to honor their creative impulses to move, try, reach, and get…everything!

Toddlers have no other choice than to push. They must find their boundaries by thrusting outward into the world. They often find their edges by pushing off ours, which can be messy and painful for teachers sometimes, especially if we didn't mine our own Treasure of Independence at two years of age. Yet that is the nature of individuation: they push off us, so we must be the stability that allows them to propel into the world. Ouch for us, but it's the job.

To become Sparkle Kids, toddlers need our Teaching and Learning focus on healthy boundaries, not limits and rules, which is what we usually ramp up at this age. Boundaries are different from limits and rules. Boundaries are containers that hold our thoughts, emotions, and desires, like our physical skin holds our muscles, bones, organs, and a lot of water. Boundaries are edges that enable us to individuate in thought, feeling, and longing/wanting. Based on my experience so far, I predict that most of you reading this need to strengthen the health of your boundaries.

Children of this age need us to respect their individuality, to see them for who they are and acknowledge it. Instead, very often, teachers tell toddlers:

- Their feelings and desires are not acceptable. ("Don't be angry." or "You don't want that! It's dirty!")
- They don't feel how they feel or know what they know. ("You don't *really* like that, do you?" or "I'm not mad," when all signs point to mad.)
- How they feel, as if the adult knows that better than the child. ("You don't hate me; you love me!") This one is just silly, when you think about it, but I know we adults do it all the time.

Notice all the don'ts? "Don't be angry. Don't want that. Don't hate." Toddlers live in a heap of No, right when they need a big old world of Yes! Don't get me wrong. Good toddler teaching is not giving in to their every whim.

Yet we must show that we hear those whims and see those passionate emotions. These little beings need to know that we see them for who *they* are, not who we wish they were, who we think we were at their age, or as some other figment of our imaginations. To become Sparkle Kids, children need teachers who respect their individuality, their uniqueness. They need us to stay with #thischildthismoment.

Our job is to support their empathy when it begins to emerge. Empathy for someone else's emotion is an early indicator of an emotional boundary. We help them by giving them language and self-awareness about their own feelings. We let them feel the power of their motivations and self-interests while teaching them not to disregard others' motivations, which may be at odds with theirs.

Independence as a Childhood Treasure is mined, cut, and polished to a luster when we know who we are. We know: 1) what we think, 2) how we feel, and 3) what we want…and are completely unashamed to express all of it. (Notice we're not supposed to rule the world with it; expressing what I want is not the same as getting it.)

An adult with Independence in the foundation of their Little Red House isn't someone who has always gotten their way. Instead, they are confident that *who they are matters* and that their unique contributions to the world have inherent value. If you don't know what that feels like, I promise, you want it for yourself as well as for the kids you teach.

No matter what age the children in your learning environment, you can support this healthy self-expression. It begins with anchoring the other side of the foundation for their Little Red House. When children add the Childhood Treasure of Independence, the floor of the safe house they are building for their personality lays Trust under one foot and Independence under the other.

Again, children don't need us to be perfect at this. A Sparkle Kid grows in a learning environment that *mostly* sees them for who they are. Remember, to be a good enough teacher is good enough.

Broken Tools

Terrible Twos. A toddler is not a brat or willful or a bully. That is the Wild Child Tamer talking. Without any time to learn finesse and with few language skills, they are expressing, for the first time, all their feelings and a brain full of electrifying thoughts and interests. We must allow their emotions and thoughts to be messy and loud while they are learning to express them and understand them.

After all, yours are messy sometimes too, right? You've been learning about your emotions for decades, and your expressions are still chaotic sometimes, so please, give them a break as they're just starting out. Allow toddlers to be diamonds in the rough for a while. Be patient in trying to understand their thinking. It is not logical yet, but it is thinking, and it means something to them.

Manners and Sharing. Just don't. This is not the age. Yes, toddlers are a bit wild and anarchic. Yes, they don't seem to notice their impact on others. Yes, they take things and bite and hit. Thus, the Anti-Sparkle Plan cornerstone of the Tamer. Still, this is not the age at which to punish these behaviors as if they were intentionally malicious by trying to enforce a set of expectations more developmentally appropriate for older children. The Boss-of-You strategy can force this structure on toddlers, but they won't understand it.

Toddlers are in the process of losing their egocentrism, but they haven't lost it all yet. They cannot say "please" and "thank you" with any understanding of humility or gratitude. That comes later. "I'm sorry" means absolutely nothing to them and is repeated only as a meaningless, rote phrase when required by adults. Of course, model politeness. *You* say please, thank you, and I'm sorry. They're always watching.

When teachers force toddlers to use manners, the message the child receives is that what they really feel in that moment is irrelevant, and they still won't feel sorry or grateful. Ask to be moved to a classroom with threes and fours if you want to see these skills for politeness and humility develop.

Also, toddlers are biologically incapable of sharing. It's theirs and you'll never convince them it isn't, no matter what the IT is. So, get more building blocks and dolls in your toddler classroom because sharing is not a natural part of this development stage.

You may want to read some of the many books about teacher responses to biting, hitting, and snatching toys that will teach the interpersonal lessons of "what is me/what is not me" and eventually enable kindnesses like manners and sharing. Sometimes, with our Broken Tools from Taming and Bossing, we inadvertently convert toddlers' truly unintentional aggressions into real bullying down the road.

Physical Punishment and Time-out. Again, just don't. First, physical punishment of any age child is an abuse of power by adults. Period. That's why it's outlawed in most educational environments and in all of those run or overseen by local and state governments. If you want to hear some horror stories about how children are treated in unregulated environments, ask me. I can go on for hours. Here, I'll just mention the toddler whose thumbs were bound together with duct tape so she wouldn't suck them. True story, circa 1996.

Spanking and other forms of physical punishment are old, outmoded holdovers from our country's Germanic-European roots. Hitting children to teach them dates back centuries when we did not know about early development or that 95 percent of the brain is built after birth. Now we know better, so we do better.

Hitting children—or grabbing and pulling on their arms or shoulders to control them—doesn't teach them to behave, especially at this tender age. It teaches them only this: it's okay to manhandle and hurt people who are smaller and weaker than you.

Physical punishment of a toddler (yes, even a swat to "get their attention") is unnecessary and unhelpful to your cause as an educator. If you can't figure out any other way to get the attention of a toddler than hitting them, then either ask to work with older kids or consume more professional development. Education is not about control at any age, but especially with toddlers.

The nonphysical punishment known as time-out is also ineffective with toddlers. This term is an abbreviation of behavioral psychologist B. F. Skinner's original term, "time out from positive reinforcement." The principle of the time-out procedure is to eliminate the possibility of reward as a consequence for a specific behavior. We know it works if it reduces the occurrence of that behavior.

Huh?

This basic lesson is Behavioral Science 101. For example, a hungry rat in a Skinner box has already learned from many repetitions that pressing a bar leads to food pellets. Yum. Rat enthusiastically presses bar and receives many food pellets. Rat joy.

Occasionally, rat stops pressing bar and randomly does some other ratty things. Upon standing on its hind legs to sniff up higher (a very ratty thing), the lights go out, a buzzer sounds, and the food bar locks for some time before the lights come back on and the food bar again begins to operate.

While the box is dark and the bar is locked, rat is in the condition known as "time-out" from its positive reinforcement of food pellets. No matter how many times it presses the bar in the dark, there is no food and no rat joy. After a few dozen repetitions of this whole sequence—rat stands up, buzzer sounds and lights go out, no rat joy for a while—rat no longer stands on its hind legs to sniff high. We have "punished" that behavior out of its ratty repertoire. Time-out worked!

I hate to liken a human child to a rat in a Skinner box, but as soon as we apply the technology of behavior modification to children, we do that. (Trivia tidbit: In U.S. education and parenting cultures, behavior modification has been the source of our predominant teaching and discipline strategies for generations.) The truth is, at the toddler stage of development, a child is almost as random as the rat in its behavior.

Toddlers move fast and are pretty unpredictable, right? So, linking a period of time-out to a particular behavior from that fast-moving stream is tricky. Their ability to understand a verbal explanation for why they're in time-out is still limited. A toddler may have no idea why they are sitting in semi-isolation while others get all the access to the teachers and other toys.

And then there's this fact: semi-isolation is not truly time-out. If the "toddler joy" you're removing as reinforcement is participation in the social environment, you can't make it stop operating for a couple of minutes like the food bar. The flood of positive reinforcement from the environment is impossible to turn all the way off for children sitting on the sidelines. A child in a corner chair sometimes has the best seat in the house as observer of the whole human drama in the early childhood classroom.

As teachers, we must also be aware that the classroom environment may not truly be rewarding for a toddler. When we remove a child from the social environment for time-out, it's on the assumption that they are rewarded by the social environment, that they are "hungry" for it, as the rat is hungry for food. Are they, though? I think toddlers are still egocentric enough that, if all the other kids disappeared, they'd probably be happy about being alone with all the toys and teachers for quite a while before they missed their playmates. The social environment may not yet be reinforcing enough for time-out to be an effective punishment for toddlers.

Finally, at this age, our teaching needs to be focused on helping children see the effects of their behavior on others. We need to start drawing the lines of connection between their actions and the consequences for others. They won't truly understand cause and effect for a few years, but this is where the learning begins.

Making these connections is how we begin to pull them out of egocentrism. Teachers need to help them see the realities of living in a community. Removing them from the arena of their offense to sit alone doesn't help a child learn that a particular action has undesirable impacts on others. No matter how much you talk about it, they will not understand it as well as if they have to face the children who are hurt or upset by their actions.

Basic Tools

All the Basic Tools for mining the Treasure of Independence come from the same toolbox because they are all about fostering emotional intelligence. These tools ask you, teacher, to #benewbebrave. Even those of you with master's degrees in Early Education may not have learned all this in your studies.

Emo Lingo. Young toddlers can't yet think about their emotions. They feel them physically in their bodies but have no words yet to label these feelings—physical sensations—in their muscles, digestive system, and nervous system. Our job is to provide them with the language to describe their feelings. Our job is to respectfully mirror those feelings back to them in compassionate and empathetic words, to increase self-awareness and self-acceptance.

First, we need to use the strategy of #slowdowntunein to see the first signs of the tightening fist or quivering chin, or maybe even hear the churning gut. We cannot live inside the toddler's skin with them, to feel the physical sensations of their emotions. Yet we can often see the external signs if we're paying close attention.

Then we move toward the Emo Lingo by acknowledging the physicality. "I see your chin is trembling and your eyes filling with tears. Do you feel that?" Inviting the child into more awareness of their bodily sensations supports their construction of the "me/not me" emotional boundary. When we follow up with, "Are there other feelings inside your body?" we invite that self-awareness to expand, and we may also give ourselves more information about #thischildthismoment as their little hands clutch a churning tummy.

Finally, we teach for learning, starting with small words for small people: "These feelings in your body—tears in your eyes, trembling chin, and upset tummy—might be the feelings of being sad." Maybe not all at once in a verbal flood, but in sips and drops as opportunities allow, we might add: "Sad means missing something that is not here. It means wishing for something that I'm not having now. It means not happy with how things are."

Emo Express. Toddlers also need some Teaching and Learning to express emotion in healthy ways. Our pedagogical history of "teaching" a healthy emotional intelligence is that we haven't. Up until now, we have sorted and sifted emotions into categories of acceptable and not. We have assigned them as appropriate for one gender but not another. We have learned to feel comfortable with some feelings but not others.

Up until now, we have always helped toddlers express some emotions—the acceptable, gender-relevant ones that don't make us uncomfortable—but not all of the emotions, not all of *their* emotions. The result has been generations of children and adults who know how to express some emotions in healthy ways but bottle up or act out others. How can teaching influence the learning of emotional expression?

The Emo Lingo is the point of entry here, too. Using the language of emotion, which is all mental, we talk with toddlers about the physical experience and also the expression of those feelings. We always begin with the body, describing the expression of feelings as we witness it. "You are pounding the air with your fists and stomping your feet on the ground. It looks like you are expressing mad. Are you feeling mad?"

Keep the Emo Lingo simple at this age; toddlers are Mad, Sad, Glad, Afraid, or Calm. There is room later to build out the sophistication of various states of Mad, from peeved or frustrated to enraged or outraged, and to learn all the ways to feel calm, quiet, restful, peaceful. That will be good vocabulary development for fours, fives, and beyond.

The second component of the Emo Express curriculum is to offer forms of expression when needed. Perhaps a child is stuck, frustrated by an inability to express those physical feelings. Perhaps another child needs new ways to express feelings that work better in the classroom community. What we teach is that punching the pillow is an okay way to express Mad, whereas punching your friend is not. Mad, Sad, and Afraid and their expression are never the problem. It's the form of expression that we must guide as we utilize #benewbebrave in our teaching.

Showing the Impact. A third teaching tool for children's expansion of emotional intelligence is to help them see the impact of their behavior on others, without shaming them for it. "Oh, look! Our friend, Sharice, is crying! She is sad because you took the baby doll she was playing with. Please give Sharice that doll, and then you can have one of these three babies over here." No need to solicit a fake apology they don't understand, and no need to make them feel sad too. Help them see their impact and make restitution. Provide an alternative. Distract them—it's the easiest thing in the world with a toddler!

The point is to help children notice how we make a difference to other people, how we have an effect on the world with our behavior. Of course, be sure to point out the positives too! "Jared, look how Cosi is laughing now! She is so happy because you hugged her!" "Jermaine does not look so afraid now that you are holding his hand."

How Does It Feel? Finally, we teach children to recognize emotion in others, to support their naturally occurring empathy. There is no need to teach empathy. Young children feel it automatically as they find their emotional boundary. Once they understand that the feelings someone else is having are different from their own, empathy is born. Our teaching only needs to support their learning to recognize Mad, Sad, Glad, Afraid, and Calm in someone else.

There are dozens of wonderful picture books to introduce children to how various emotional states appear in others. There are also many commercial classroom materials with drawn faces or photographs of emotional expressions. Use those, if you like, to get started. However, it is the faces and bodies of real people that tell the most accurate stories of the emotions within. Learning to see evidence of emotion that invokes empathy requires nothing more than a community of friends who #slowdowntunein to one another. Presence and attention beget empathy.

Speaking of empathy…remember, toddlers are living through the most terrible betrayal of their lives, learning they are not the center of the universe. We each must come through that change and still feel that we're okay as we are. Yet, how can I be okay as I am if I'm no longer the center of the universe but just one star dancing among billions? Isn't that a demotion? If you could remember facing this shocking truth in your own life, you'd know what a rough ride this is for every toddler. Be compassionate and supportive.

No matter what age the children in your classroom, you can support healthy self-expression of emotion and help them anchor their Little Red Houses sturdily with the Childhood Treasure of Independence. You can, that is, if you've mined your own Independence and found your own boundaries. This is the classroom in which teachers may most deeply need to #staysanebeyourself.

The Explosion of Faith

By three years of age, the driver of Maturation is initiative. The young child has finally noticed the world beyond their own egocentric self and started giving birth to Big Dreams that will change the world for the better.

Faith
Maturation driver—Initiative; Big Dreams
Construction driver—Can I believe in myself?

Starting at about thirty months of age, and continuing until almost four years, children discover that there is a world of amazing possibility out there. Their two-year focus on finding a Me—knowing all its needs, emotions, and longings—seems to end abruptly one day when the older toddler lifts their head, looks around, and says, "Hey, wait. All *this*, too?"

Newly coordinated motor control and early speech enable play, first with adults and then with other children, in a somewhat interactive process. At first, play is more about being side by side in parallel but noninteractive activity. Play evolves to be truly interactive and cooperative by age four. Imagination flourishes at three, and the fantasy world of this young child gives birth to Big Dreams.

In this maturational window of opportunity, the child's Construction driver for meaning and understanding is the question of whether they can believe in themselves and their Big Dreams. How teachers respond to children's rich fantasy life and faith (which I define as the belief in something—anything—beyond the existence of proof) teaches them whether their capacity for dreaming is valid and relevant for the rest of us. They need adults whose Teaching and Learning focus is on imagination and pretending (role-play)—or what is called the "willingness to suspend disbelief."

That term from the world of theater fits perfectly in this context. Most of us adults were long ago taught *disbelief*—had it drilled into us, usually starting at this young age of three, sadly. Our lesson often was, "Your Big Dreams and role-play for your future life are not only irrelevant to me, they are funny or ridiculous—something by which I am amused and entertained, and something I might mock and poke fun at."

Even without these cruelties, our adult default is often to doubt the existence of that which is beyond our sphere of awareness. Threes never doubt. They BELIEVE—just like that, in all caps—with all their heart, all their mental power, and from the depths of their soul.

For your consideration, have you ever seen this illustration?

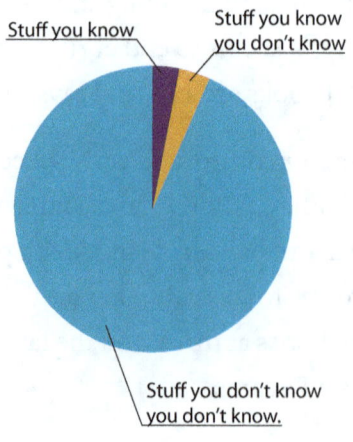

As teachers, we must remember this reality that there is much more we don't know compared to what we do know. We must learn to respect the reality depicted here and practice suspending our *trained* disbelief of everything outside the two small "Stuff You Know" slices. We must allow ourselves to fall into children's fantasies, let go of feeling foolish as we pretend to do and be what we "know" isn't "real."

I invite you to let the children see you interact with their imagination in ways that validate it and them. You needn't believe in fairies or aliens to support a child's mining of the Childhood Treasure of Faith, but as a teacher for this age child, you must believe in the value of their belief. Let me say that in a different way: You must believe that fantasy and role-play are significant brain builders. Threes take their faith in the unseen very seriously—however they dream within that very large segment of the chart in the "You Don't Know" slices. They need teachers who do the same.

Broken Tools

Get Real. This tool comes straight from the Boss-of-You cornerstone of the Anti-Sparkle Plan. Three-year-old children do not need a dose of hard, cold reality. They don't need to wake up to your adult view of the world. To be more effective with that kind of teaching, be sure to temper it with huge doses of empathy and compassion and apply it around age six or seven instead.

Threes don't need to be told to stop believing in the impossible. Do most adults tell a three-year-old to stop believing in the Tooth Fairy, Easter Bunny, or Santa Claus? Some do, but not most; in fact, three is the age at which adults usually begin to spin these fantasies for children. Yet many teachers of threes seem to have no qualms declaring to children that their plans to create something brand new or to change the world in some amazing way are beyond what can be done.

I love to hear teachers speak honestly to three-year-old children who are proposing the apparently impossible by saying, "I have no idea how to help you with that," rather than "You can't do that." Oh, I also love to hear them add, "Let's see if we can figure it out together."

Over-Resourcing Imagination. This Broken Tool is common in preschool and child care classrooms. Here's the bottom line: Children of three do not need a physical object to represent every single thing they might want to play about.

For example, when children want to pretend there is food on a plate, they do not need a plastic piece of pretend food. In fact, I believe their play and learning experience is better if they don't have one. Empty cans and pots and pans on the shelves, yes. Pretend food? Without it, they'll either visualize it with the same parts of their brain that are activated by the senses—imagining they see, smell, and taste it—or they'll find some object to represent the food, such as a square wooden block. The plastic stuff doesn't look right anyway, and it sure doesn't smell or taste like anything other than plastic and kids.

I'll tell you a little family secret. As tween girls, my two sisters and I built elaborate penthouse apartments for our Barbie dolls using family room furniture, cardboard boxes, and wooden blocks, among other "recyclables" in our home, because none of our three Barbies owned a Barbie DreamHouse. My mother's fancy 1960s high-heeled bedroom slippers (envision mules with sequins and feathers on the toes) served as sports cars in the absence of the pink plastic one sold by Mattel. We even made our dolls' clothes (yes, with a sewing machine) because the price per outfit at the local TG&Y store was beyond our means. Are you surprised to hear that the building of the penthouses was easily two-thirds of our play and fun? We three sisters shared a bedroom, and there was no absence of bickering among us upstairs. But down in the family room, in imagination land, we got along terrifically. A plastic house and furniture and a wardrobe full of purchased outfits would have robbed us of all that.

Children do not need more *stuff* to play with. They need Faith—imagination, pretend, dreams—and they need *us*. They need us to engage with them in developing imaginary worlds out of the junk from our own world. They need us to act as if we're eating the imaginary food as if at the lunch table. Mmmmm! Delicious!

They need us to give them open-ended, creative play materials like blocks, old clothes and shoes, and interesting junk from garage sales. They need blankets and tables and pillows, empty cardboard boxes, lengths of fabric, and other nonspecific stimulants to creativity. A blanket is only a blanket as long as it's not the roof of a fort.

Wait until you see what they do with less! Simply provide a few basic materials and allow them to add the wealth of ALL they can imagine. Don't limit them to the stories provided by plastic food, pretend carpentry tools, or premade costumes. Want to really #benewbebrave? Take the children out into the woods with nothing but their bare hands in their pockets, a trowel and ball of twine in yours (and the first aid kit and emergency contacts in your backpack, of course), and be amazed by what they can build when given safely loose reins on their activity.

Too School-y. The time on the clock, your printed schedule on the wall, and your plans for use of the carpeted area during circle time are as irrelevant to a three's imaginary world as that world is to your need for snack to start on time. For this reason, threes need a learning environment that has some flexibility in its schedule and use of space. Nonnegotiable time limits and restrictions on how to use the available space can work for older children and youth—age eight or nine and up—but are not developmentally aligned with the Maturation and Construction drivers at the age of three.

Basic Tools

Optimum Flexibility. At any age, children need more space and time; I can't think of a child I've met who had enough. Particularly around age three, though, they are deeply emotionally attached to many of the creations pouring out of them. They sometimes want time to continue, beyond your schedule's borders, until they reach the point *they* define as the finish. Older children will achieve enough self-governance to cope with their frustration; threes don't have it yet.

Thus, transitions from one piece of the schedule to the next are most successful for threes when somewhat incremental. That is, some children, who are ready, make the transition earlier, while others trail along at the end of a little window of time. Threes also need strategies to sustain protected space for a project to be continued later. Signage (e.g., "Do Not Touch" written in the child's own hand) or transferring the partially completed project to a sheltered spot can allow for a child's investment of energy to spread over the course of a day or even across several days.

Not all long-term projects are possible. That occasional "no" is easier to swallow if you've been fed a steady diet of "yes" most of the time. As always, there is no need to be perfect with any of these tools. Be as consistent as you can be. Become more ego-ware and self-governed in your own S.E.L.F. and strive, always, to be ever-more consistent with your accommodations to children's need for space and time. Relax into "yes" as much as you can. In fact…

The Answer to How Is Yes. This title from Peter Block's great 2001 book for business leaders is incredibly apt as a motto for teachers of three-year-olds. Teachers of this age group must start responding with more Yes to children's "impossible" dreams.

Once upon a time, some children of four and five worked with their teachers to solve the problem of how to draw a *life-size* picture of a brontosaurus. This is not a fairytale, so think about that for a second—a life-size brontosaurus, as in seventy-two feet from nose to tail. Are you surprised to learn that they accomplished this goal, or that another group of kids this age designed and built a little water park for the birds nesting near their school? Both stories are true, and as you'd expect, both groups had the help of teachers and parents. Together, they found Yes after Yes for the children's ideas and interests.

Answer me this: Would fours and fives have figured out projects such as these if, when they were three, their teachers replied to similar suggestions with, "Oh, honey, you can't do that. You're too little." Even unintentionally thoughtless but imagination-dampening teacher statements such as, "But I can't pretend to be a boy; I'm a girl," may further bury the Childhood Treasure of Faith. Back in the 1970s, teachers told preschooler boys they couldn't grow up to be mommies, and girls that they couldn't grow up to be daddies. Maybe some still tell them those lies, but it turns out we were wrong about that.

When faced with a three's inventions and dreams, I invite you to replace the thousand frantic How questions in your mind with the simplicity of Yes. You may have been taught that, as teacher, you need to know all the answers—all the ways to do. But you don't know them and can't, so you must #benewbebrave. Yes, of course we can try to do that, whatever impossible thing your little three-year-old imagination just conjured! Yes. I don't know how, either, but let's try. Yes. Where should we begin?

You may wonder why you should tackle impossible dreams with children so young their speech can barely be understood. Two reasons are primary: 1) so they will learn that dreams have value and should always be pursued, and 2) the process of trying is a journey teeming with opportunities to learn.

That's right! Any of your curriculum's learning objectives for threes—all the state education goals, Head Start standards, or whatever structure shapes your learning environment—all your objectives can be woven into activity evolving from a child's impossible idea. Whether successful in the end or not, the striving toward a child's dream will create a stronger learning community and offer opportunities to develop all the skills, knowledge, and dispositions that matter.

If this way of teaching seems a bit strange, study The Project Approach or the Reggio Emilia model of early childhood to build your understanding and skills. The kids don't need you to be an expert on all this right now. Just start saying Yes more and let your Teaching and Learning intention for imagination and creativity expand from that beginning.

Negotiation by the Boxes

The Maturation driver at four is for order, for the rule of law. These children are seemingly aware that a three's endless expansion into

> **Negotiation**
> Maturation driver—Law and order
> Construction driver—Can I get along with others?

Yes may not be all we need. Clearly, they eventually conclude, we also need some No!

Fours become very committed to the rules, laws, structure, predictability, and expectations held by others. Their actual purpose, I believe, is to figure out the loopholes. That sounds more devious than the motivation behind it.

Fours are now learning how to get along inside the limits and agreements imposed upon them by negotiating for what they want *within* those borders. They do want order, but also, they want to understand how that structure can still yield what they want. They learn all this at the subconscious level, for the most part. Even at four, kids are not intentionally manipulating teachers!

Here's what they are doing. Fours are constructing new understandings about how limits and agreements form a sort of "box" that contains all their choices in that moment, like a toy box contains their toys. In their neural network, they are building strategies for negotiating through life's limits and agreements. This is the age at which we all start trying to get along in life's sandboxes, playing inside these metaphoric boxes full of choices.

This is the age at which a child becomes aware that they need relationships. (They have needed them all along, of course, but they are just starting to figure that out intellectually.) Their egocentrism, up to this point, has still been strong. Other people have been mostly experienced as tools to use or barriers to be removed. Though children play "together" at three, true cooperative interaction in play comes along at four.

Whereas our plaintive cry as teachers might be, "Can't we all just get along?" the questions driving a four-year-old's construction of social understanding are more personal: Can I get along? Can *relationships with others* be the source for getting what I want, the route to optimize my potential? If so, how does that work?

Building from the foundation of the Treasure of Independence, children should consistently be aware of all their boundaries by late-four.

Boundary awareness emerges over time, roughly in this order: children first learn they have a body and others have separate bodies (by one year); then that their emotions are separate from others' emotions (around two years); third that their longings, desires, and wants are likewise uniquely theirs (about three). One of the last remnants of the no-boundary perspective should disappear at this new stage. At around four years, kids discover the mental boundary that separates their cognitive point of view. They learn that their memories and thoughts are theirs alone.

The first indicator that a mental boundary is containing a child's personal point of view is quite literally a shift in viewpoint—in visual perspective. Before the mental boundary is located, children operate from the apparent assumption that you can see what they can see. If there is something that they can see from their position (point of view) but you cannot see it, they don't seem to know that. They perceive it, so they think you do too. For example, one of you is looking at the front side of a cereal box and the other is looking at the back side. Assuming you can see it, the child is asking you about something on their side of the box. A mental boundary erases such behavior.

The mental, or cognitive, boundary is the one needed for the child's construction of true relationships at age four. Full and healthy boundaries are what allow each person in a relationship to be the individual they are. Up until now, every other person in relationship with a child was simply some form of projection of the child's internal world. (Sidebar here: Can you see how messy teacher–child relationships can become with children projecting themselves onto you, and you—maybe never having found all your boundaries—still projecting yourself onto the children?)

Four-year-old kids need your Teaching and Learning focus, broadly, to be on building community. Specifically, they need help clarifying and understanding the kinds of limits and agreements that create a functional community—in this case, a classroom community. For young fours, a functional community will still mean functional for them.

From a sole focus on whether they can get what they want, they will grow in awareness. By five or six, they will understand that giving some attention to a community good is not just good because it's better for them. By six, they begin to feel the reward of giving to a larger purpose than self. The seed of empathy in a toddler's Independence pushes up early green shoots at age four that fully blossom into altruism at six.

At first, though, fours are still mostly about themselves. When it comes to being diplomatic about their interests, fours hold onto a bit of that "diamond in the rough" status from being three. Therefore, a focus on community with fours also means a focus on problem solving.

I am delicately saying, there will be conflict. Maybe not blood, but certainly conflict. Every single day with fours, there will be conflict. Gird your loins, teacher, or should I say, your boundaries? Yes. Gird your boundaries! This is a classroom in which #staysanebeyourself is a crucial cornerstone.

Truly, this is the age at which a functional community can be born in a classroom when artful teachers, who are also healthy human beings, are in charge. Without our own healthy boundaries, though, this is also the age in which power struggles can become truly challenging and more dangerous. People *can* get hurt. Power struggles with fours, in which we sound more like another preschooler than the teacher, are one of the Broken Tools we sometimes use with this age group.

This age group is the one that requires teachers to polish up their own Treasure of Independence as well as sharpen the facets of their skills for Negotiation in life's boxes of limits and agreements. When the teacher exercises the power of choice and personal agency in their own life, they can offer children those same experiences.

Fours have all the skills and prerequisite motivation, from their maturational evolution, to create cooperative community. Their Construction driver is getting along with others. So, why is it that this is also the age at which children become attached to the culture of competition, in board and card games that create winners and losers, team sports with points that create winners and losers, and a seeming obsession with being *first*—in line, to be called on, to get the snack to pass, whatever can be done first, rather than second or—worst of all—*last*. Being last becomes a great catastrophe in life at age four.

Perhaps counterintuitively, this need for competition and winning is an important aspect of developing the arts of negotiation and getting along. However, especially within the culture of the United States, it badly needs some balancing with a culture of cooperation. This is the age at which we can notice, increase self-awareness about, and become adept at a healthy balance between competition and cooperation.

Great teachers of fours use teaching tools that help children's development of that delightful balance. The Teaching and Learning focus in their work blends a healthy and compassionate competition in games with healthy and empathetic community cooperation in work.

Boundaries that recognize our uniqueness and separateness are not intended to isolate us in a dog-eat-dog competition to be better than everyone else. Here at age four is where kids learn to expand beyond their respect for the unique self that they are. Finally, they begin to develop equal respect for the other unique selves around them. Maturation opened a mine shaft to Negotiation, and we find interpersonal respect at the heart of this raw ore. You can't "teach" interpersonal respect to a toddler, no matter how you guide, praise, or punish them. They just aren't ready yet, but fours are vibrating with maturational readiness for this Teaching and Learning.

Broken Tools

Impose Structure. From the yearning to avoid conflict, imposition of rules and routines is a common strategy in four-year-old classrooms. For example, the number of children in an activity center is restricted with a chart system to prevent conflicts that occur when too many children try to play in a too-small space or with too few materials. Children are required to walk from point A to point B in straight lines, keeping their hands to themselves, to avoid conflicts during transitions. Teachers impose long lists of rules and add to them as new misbehaviors occur. As each new disruption arises, a new rule is written to prohibit it. Fours are then punished for infractions of rules with a time-out or loss of a "privilege" such as outdoor play (which is developmentally essential, not a privilege).

Power Struggles. Teachers often find themselves embroiled in power struggles with children of this age as they strive to maintain the control required by an inherited I-Am-the-Boss-of-You strategy from the Anti-Sparkle Plan. Unfortunately, to maintain this unnatural relationship, we must begin to tell children lies—usually well-intentioned or "funny" ones, to begin with. Here is a small sample of such lies, told to me when I was a child or offered by other parents and teachers:

- "I once knew a girl who liked to stick her tongue out like that. She did it so much that one day, her tongue got stuck out and she couldn't put it back in."

- "You have to use the bathroom here because they don't have bathrooms at the store."
- "If you swallow those watermelon seeds, you'll wind up with one growing in your stomach."
- "If you pinch your friend one more time, I'll have to call the police to come arrest you."

The lies are a problem in themselves, and that problem is doubled when lies are used to win a power struggle with a child (#2 on this list was such a lie).

By age four, kids can often tell when we're lying to them. Something about there being no bathrooms at the store just doesn't ring true anymore, whereas they may have believed such a lie at age three. Fours stop "caving in" to the teacher's will when faced with such dire and fallacious promises because they no longer believe us. They stop cooperating with our Bossing and begin resisting. Remember the difference between the willing and the resister in the graphic on p. 33?

From my perspective, our loss of control over them is far less important than their loss of faith in us. In our efforts to keep children "in line," we have surrendered the imprimatur of honesty as well as the high moral ground. Always before children are fully grown, they come to understand that the teachers they once saw as infallible and perfect deities are only human. Why pull yourself down from the pedestal any sooner by acting without integrity?

Yes, you can get away with it for a while. When the day comes that such lies lose their efficacy to "win" in a power struggle, it will turn out you have lost way more than that battle of the moment. You will have lost a substantial and critical component of a healthy relationship between teacher and child. An even greater sorrow is that the child will carry an expectation of dishonesty into their relationship with the next teacher, and the next.

Impose Leadership. Another Broken Tool children receive from teachers, when we lean too far toward the Boss-of-You strategy in the Anti-Sparkle Plan, is the imposition of our own leadership structure on the group. We assign leadership roles, such as Line Leaders and Team Captains. We appoint peer helpers: "José, please fasten Janette's shoe for her."

Without our imposed structure, and with our trust and support, natural leadership can emerge in a group, giving every child an opportunity to try out leadership in a way that works for them. We invite awareness of the need—"Who can help Janette fasten her shoe?"—and natural helpers emerge. We can also empower children to ask others for help, to trust other members of the community with their needs: "Janette, which friend would you like to ask for help fastening your shoe?"

Promote Competition. The most Broken Tool we use with fours is the promotion of competition for competition's sake, with an emphasis on winning/being first/being best as the most important feature of that competition. For a long time in our country, our predominant cultural model for both social interaction and economics has been based on competition, and we cannot pretend that away.

However, I will argue that competition "wins" best and gains most when it occurs in the context of a community. An individual win can also lift a whole group. The two outcomes are not mutually exclusive. We should not put children into "dog-eat-dog" competition when they are brand new at learning to get what they want. We do them a long-term disservice by ignoring the impact on community cohesion when one person wins and everyone else loses.

Basic Tools

At four years old, children are looking for their "birthright authority." They don't need ALL the power, just what is rightfully theirs. They want decision-making authority in their lives, over actions such as where they sit, what they wear, who their friends are, and how they spend time.

The tools needed to mine the Childhood Treasure of Negotiation are those that honor, and teach healthy use of, personal authority. Of course, at this young age, children still need lots of shared authority with older and wiser partners in life. For teachers, this is the age child for whom we must begin to relinquish more of our authority as we focus on teaching them to use theirs well.

Clear Communication. In my Development Do-Overs on the Treasure of Negotiation, I use a metaphor of "Choice Boxes" comprised of Limits we set and Agreements we forge with our relationship partners. When children are four years old, one of the best tools we can offer them is clear language that defines these boxes for them.

When we help make children's choices visible to them, they learn more quickly how to negotiate within the boxes that define those choices. The strategy to #benewbebrave calls upon you to enter the child's world and find their level of understanding about negotiation. Can you see how they see their choices? How do they learn to weigh one option against another and choose wisely? Can you learn to see the power dynamics that contain their options as *they* see them?

Clarify the language of choice and negotiation for children even more as you #staysanebeyourself. Do your mining work on this Treasure if it wasn't done fully when you were four. Become more Ego-aware and Self-governed in your adult decisions to better understand how children are learning what you now take for granted.

Make sure you understand the limitations and agreements that shape your decision-making processes today. Learn to artfully use the language of Agreements and Limits, helping children fully understand their choices and how to make them in ways that enhance their lives and the communities in which they live—family, neighborhood, and classroom.

Community Meetings. What if gathering together as a classroom community, in one big circle, was not always for a lesson in the language of a calendar or for practice at identifying rhyming words or even to listen to a great storybook? What if "circle time" with fours also focused on learning to get along with the people in the circle?

What if this unique community of people—children and adults together—met regularly to talk about how things are going? With your Seek Sparkle & Shine Plan strategies of #thischildthismoment and #seethemnotyou, can you allow the children to create interpersonal dialogue and decisions that work for all of you? Can you give them this level of shared personal authority as community authority?

Imagine this: Rather than deciding on your own to limit the highly desirable block center to four children with a poster and clothespins, or some other management tool, you ask the community of children what to do. You invite them to define the problem and create *their* solutions for it.

If you're thinking, "Yeah, right! Turn circle time over to the kids...that would be crazy," I offer the following script to facilitate your imagination. This scenario assumes several months of experience with community conversations, so these children are all raising their hands to speak and waiting for their turns, at least most of the time.

> **Teacher:** Now is our three minutes for sharing problems or challenges we're facing here in our community. Who has a share?

Child 1: Jeremy knocked down my block tower.
Teacher: Jeremy knocked down blocks.
Child 2: Yeah, and Merced knocked mine!
Teacher: Merced knocked down blocks.
Child 3 (Merced): No! I did that on accident!
Teacher: Merced knocked down blocks by accident. How did that happen, Merced?
Merced: I only stood up, but his blocks were too close. I bumped them on accident.
Teacher: Sounds like it was crowded in blocks today. Any other shares about challenges in blocks?

Imagine this conversation goes on for another two or three minutes until all the concerns about crowding in blocks are aired and the children come to understand that there are sometimes too many children playing with blocks in the space available. They may even see that four children is a number that works, but five or more creates crowding and problems.

The second part of your challenge to #seethemnotyou is to ask for their solutions to the problem they have identified.

Teacher: What are some ways we could solve this problem of the block play area being too crowded when more than four children play at the same time?
Child 3: Make more room for blocks.
Teacher: Make more room. What else?
Child 2: Yeah, more room for blocks!
Teacher: That's two who like the idea of more room for blocks. What else?
Child 1: Maybe only three friends at a time in blocks.
Teacher: Only small groups of friends play in blocks; maybe three. What else?

As the brainstorming conversation continues, all the good ideas and some wild ones come up. Because every classroom has at least one child who will suggest something like it, maybe you join the children in a belly laugh at the idea of the whole classroom being for block play all day ("Where and when would we have snack or lunch?"). Yet each idea is honored by inclusion in the list for consideration. (Trust the community not to adopt wild ideas and relax in the knowledge that you can always gently and openly pull rank, as Responsible Adult, if you have to.)

Perhaps in a few minutes, the group intent starts to gel around one or two of the more feasible and effective solutions. The children shift to discussing pros and cons for these two options. The passionate advocates plea the case for each alternative. If you think a group of twenty four-year-old children are not capable of this discussion, then you really haven't seen fours in all their glory. They revel in this stuff!

As teachers, our job shifts pleasantly away from saying what is what to facilitating a respectful interaction and fostering a healthy group decision-making process that includes everyone and listens to every perspective. At four, children can even learn about democracy. Allow them to vote with their feet ("Stand over here if you want a bigger block area by making a smaller science area, and stand over here if you want to keep the areas we have but limit to four the number of friends who play in blocks at the same time.").

To foster the mining of the Treasure of Negotiation, we become teachers of community relationship rather than authoritarian enforcers of our rules. We give the rest of the community a voice and help them value every voice. This is one key to a classroom of individuals becoming a functioning community, and this is the age for it.

When children are the ones who define which behaviors are a problem for them, they care more and hold each other more accountable to the rules. Very quickly, they begin to remind each other of the rules, increasing their capacity for self-governance as they do. Any child is empowered to call out a peer who is not adhering to the limits and agreements of the community. As they create their own interpersonal solutions, fewer minor infractions rise to the level of our teacherly attention.

Granted, this approach to teaching requires you, the teacher, to be flexible, to #benewbebrave. On this occasion, you might need to allow a larger block area and smaller science area. I assure you, the educational rewards in the social and emotional realm are greater than the sacrifice of your control over space design. Also—knowing fours—they will want a bigger science area again in a few weeks (especially if you add something intriguing to it!).

Children power through their mining of the Treasure of Negotiation in such an environment of group decision-making. Sharing the challenges faced in a classroom and owning them, as a whole group, encourages each child's clear thinking about what they want.

Being solution-oriented also teaches them how to get what they want through respectful communication that includes and honors others' needs. At four years, children can even come up with that list of classroom rules that guide the whole group every day.

Community-Created Rules. Rather than giving children our rules as their template for behavior and interaction, a whole new world of classroom community opens when we use #thischildthismoment and #seethemnotyou strategies from the Seek Sparkle & Shine Plan.

Think about it. How could the rules for last year's class—a completely different group of children with a teacher one year younger and less experienced—work for this new group of children? If you've been using the same set of rules for years, with each new and unique community, you've been missing one of the great joys of teaching, in my opinion.

Imagine what might happen when you invite *these* children, in *this* combination, at *this* time and place, to design agreements and limits (aka rules) for *this* community of people who live together for a few hours every day. Acknowledge the uniqueness of who they are, both as individuals and as a group. You will be amazed at what can result when children are given greater authority in the guidance of a community in which they feel ownership.

Your role as the teacher, then, shifts from Ultimate Authority to Wise Advisor, working at the edges of the crowd rather than from center stage. Your greater knowledge and experience now help them reframe their "diamond in the rough" community rules into positive teaching guidance.

- "We are gentle with our hands and feet" tells us what to do. As a rule, it teaches rather than prohibits, as in "No hitting or kicking," which is the kind of rule most fours start with. "Listen with respect" opens a door to discussions about what respect looks like, while rules such as "No interrupting" serve only to remind children of the very behavior we want to diminish.
- "Don't" and "No" rules also intensify the memory of rule infractions by triggering and building a neural network around *shame*. At four, a child's developing brain receives "interrupt" and the experience of shame at being called out for a rule infraction. The two are wired together into their neural network, but the child gains no wiring for "the behavior of *not interrupting* looks like XYZ." An agreement for "One voice at a time, with everyone listening," gives a neural pattern for what to do. It teaches without shame.

Teachers will need to #benewbebrave as children create their first list of 49 limits: no this, no that, no the other, don't do this or that. Later, teacher guidance begins to shift them from limits to agreements. "Now we know what NOT to do. How do we know what to DO?" Help them find the behaviors they can all agree are a yes! "We all agree that we should use walking feet inside. So, do we still need to have these three limits: 'No running,' 'No jumping while in line,' and 'No hopping in the room'?"

I invite you to this awareness that transformed my thinking about what education calls "classroom management": the word "discipline" comes from the same root as "disciple." When I began to see myself as building a group of followers—disciples, if you will, who praise the value and joy of learning—rather than seeing myself as a middle manager who controls wild and willful beasties, everything changed.

Peace Chairs/Mats. A significant and central use of personal authority is found in how we resolve our interpersonal conflict. Perhaps you are surprised that children of four are ready to learn to talk through conflict for a healthy win-win solution. In fact, this is the first age at which children can learn to negotiate a good for themselves that is conscious of good for others. Fours need help to learn the language of dispute resolution and restorative justice, and they have a ripeness, a readiness, for it.

Many early childhood teachers begin working with this age group by stepping in to resolve all the little fights. "She took my block!" "He won't let me play here." "They said I can't be their friend." Some come with a side of indignation, others soaked in sorrow, but these petty problems can be an endless parade to the knee of a teacher in the fours classroom. Teaching from this role, Arbiter of All Justice, is exhausting. (*Thus speaks the voice of experience*, she said with a wry smile.)

Giving children their rightful four-year-old authority to resolve such disputes requires space and time and teachers to teach good communication skills for building community. Teachers who teach children the skills of interpersonal peacemaking invest early in the needed time. Wisely, they know they'll avoid spending even more time later on those "He hit me!" and "She took my doll" moments.

I'm not spending a lot of time here teaching you how to use these Basic Tools because there are many professional development resources to teach you peace mats, child-created rules, community meetings, and using democracy as part of your classroom governance. If you want to bring these tools to your class in an artful way, you can seek more skills and knowledge through reading and other coursework. My acknowledgment page is a great resource of names to mine through Internet searches.

I hope only to convince you that the wealth buried in a four-year-old child includes the potential for a level of self-governance and community cooperation that few adults get to see. I hope to encourage you toward a desire to see more of it for yourself. I hope you can see how ready fours are for Negotiation as a gemstone of sparkling brilliance for getting along in life's sandbox. That jewel also contains the capacity for healthy competition.

Teach Competition. Teachers of fours should not simply avoid competitive games for this age group that is so ripe and ready for learning and abiding by rules. Rather, we must teach children how to compete if they are to do so with their empathy, compassion, and sense of community intact. Remember, the boundaries that come along with the Treasure of Independence at two years of age enable empathy and compassion. Boundaries allow my generous compassion for the sorrow of your loss, even as I feel the elation of the win for myself.

Part of teaching healthy and ethical competition is supporting fairness and equity in competitive play. Fours have a keen sense of fairness and "equality" but need our help to think past equal to equitable. "Is it possible for a running race to offer everyone an equal chance of winning? Jeremiah uses crutches to walk, and Nadia uses a wheelchair to move. Is a running race a fair race for our community of friends?"

Using questions to light the path for their emerging understanding is better than delivering answers. You remember something better if you have a sudden burst of insight on your own, right? So do they. We understand better when we construct meaning from within. Ask questions such as, "What is a way we ALL can move for a fair race?" rather than delivering the solution. (Then be prepared for a race by scooting on their bottoms.)

While children of four years construct their understanding of how to get along with others, their current Law and Order Maturation driver needs some balance from their Construction of "That's not me" two years ago. Remember? Their Construction driver during the mining of the Treasure of Independence was "What is me, and what is not me?"

Understanding the "not me" part of the universe includes clearly seeing others, who have feelings, thoughts, needs, and longings too. Just as I have an interior world I can share, so do you, and so does everyone. Fours are ready to understand that out there in the vastness of "not me" are a whole lot of "yous."

Teachers, then, can talk about both experiences—called winning and losing—while helping children provide community support for both experiences. Two behind-the-scenes strategies teachers can employ are to: 1) make sure that groups for competitive games change composition regularly, and 2) ensure they are relatively balanced to be potential winners.

The old approach of picking the captains and those captains pick the teams is a painful remnant of a past full of playground bullying and humiliation. Please, let go of all that tradition. Group your fours to sort the skills and talents well. Then, allow each group to decide whether they need a leader. They will appoint one from within, or one will emerge organically if they need one. Maybe they'll decide on co-captains or no captain. Every choice is a learning experience, so when teachers make all the choices, they take away opportunities to learn.

Below is some language for opening children to this balancing of Rule of Law and Compassionate Empathy. The italicized phrases are suggested #benewbebrave additions to your teaching language.

- The Cookie Monsters *earned 14 points* and the Big Birds *earned 12 points. Both groups played really hard and earned SO many points! Across both teams, we scored 26 times!*
- Which *group's* number is more points? (Demonstrate 14 more than 12, if needed, for a little math lesson.)
- Tomorrow we'll play a game where we *try to get the lowest number of points*!
- Sometimes one group *scores more points*, then the next time the other group scores more points. It's *playing fairly together* that's the most important part of the game.
- Meanwhile, we all *played hard*, had a lot of *fun*, and treated each other *fairly*.
- If we all *feel more connected/are better friends after our play*, we're doing it right!

With younger fours, for now, you can choose not to use the language of *teams* that *win* and *lose*. There will be plenty of that coming from them already, with even more later on. For now, focus on learning numerals, counting to high numbers, and relative quantities. Focus on the fun.

Discuss how it feels to belong to a community that plays well together. How does it feel to know your friends are happy for your success in the game? What is it like to be happy for them when they have even more success than you? Talk about how children help each other succeed. Cheer each other on, regardless of which group they're in. No slamming, booing, or put-downs permitted. Teachers can teach competition as a fact of life but one that doesn't have to undermine or erase our values for kindness, gratitude, connection, community, and sharing.

The Vision and the Plan

At five years, a child's Maturation driver is Competence in all the arenas of their life. Particularly, they are maturing like a blossoming flower into the capacity for *integrated* competence. That is, fives seek to be intellectually, emotionally, and physically competent, all in one flow of intention and action. The Childhood Treasure of Vision brings to light their strengths as the little strategic planners of the early childhood world.

> **Vision**
> Maturation driver—Competence
> Construction driver—Can I learn and "become"?

Fives want to know, *Can I become somebody more than I am now? Can I learn and grow in both complex and simple ways? Can I acquire new skills, knowledge, and dispositions? Can I be a different, better somebody tomorrow than I am today?*

Can you relate? Don't you want to know these things about yourself too? Don't you hope to become a kinder, better version of yourself with the passage of time? Maybe a better leader at work? Maybe a better parent at home? You can first see this drive for expanding competence in a five-year-old.

I can always tell when there's a group of five-year-old Sparkle Kids gathered. They are either taking something apart, figuring out how something works, or planning something. They plan together as a group. They listen to all the ideas and try to persuade each other toward a particular point of view or decision. Leadership voices emerge, as children "learn the ropes" in one of their earliest productivity-oriented teams. Supporting this organic learning as their teacher helps them gain capacity for success in a workplace that is still a couple of decades away.

Broken Tools

As is true with the Treasure of Faith, the least helpful tool for mining the Treasure of Vision is disbelief. Five-year-old children are full of big creative ideas that many teachers don't know how to implement. Yet with only a little bit of support, this age group can engage in sophisticated planning processes that require the use of many academic and pre-academic skills.

In many cases, fives can achieve goals that surprise adults. For example, one classroom of older Head Start children used cardboard boxes and other cardboard scrap, along with various art supplies, to create all the kinds of dwellings in which they lived. One child used a shoebox on end to be an apartment building and decorated their family's second floor apartment as it was at home. Another child used a larger boot box to create the floor plan of their single-story home. Children often pursue such goals and discover midway their idea and plans need adjusting to fit a reality they didn't understand. Even so, they have learned so much in the process of "failure" (aka "discovery") that no teacher could be sad about the outcome.

Refusal to Try. The single most dangerously dull pickaxe we hand to these little miners is our lack of willingness. It is our "that can't be done" answer to whatever Big Idea their mind has conjured up. Who says it can't? Who says you and your group of peers cannot build a sixteen-foot tower of blocks…or a sixty-foot tower of balloons? Cannot create a seventy-two-foot mural of a life-size brontosaurus? Cannot design and build a water park for little birds, with continually flowing water and fountains? Would you, as the teacher, have had the courage to say, "Yes, let's try to do that," to the groups who came up with these Big Ideas? If not, then the answer is to place your full weight on the #benewbebrave cornerstone to reach up out of refusal and into a world of Yes for your fives.

"Right" Answers = Learning. Teachers must let go of "right" answers and perfect products and fall in love with the process, for that is how humans truly learn. Most of us, from an early age, learn best by doing, trying, experimenting; by hypothesizing and rehypothesizing and tweaking that hypothesis yet again; by designing and then trying to build; by experimentation and "wrong" answers over and over and over.

What did Thomas Edison say? "I have not failed. I just found 10,000 ways that don't work." Every time it didn't work, he learned more, which led him to what is one of the greatest inventions of all time. So why are we so married to children learning and regurgitating only the "right" answers?

Brain pathways are built by interactions with people and environments, not by memorizing right answers. We want fives to wonder and ask the Big Questions that come into their lively, curious minds. We want their endless stream of *How? Why?* and *Where?*

These are not annoying distractions from our teaching. They should be its essence. These questions are children's hunger to learn. We make best use of ourselves when we help them find answers rather than providing our "right" answer. After their *How?* should come your, "I don't know, and I'd like to find that out with you! Where should we begin? What will we need to learn or think about first?"

Overstructured Activity. A corollary of this right-answer approach to teaching is overprescribing the classroom learning environment. Too many "closed" activities leave no opportunity for exploration and discovery. Rather, these teacher-planned and -directed activities hold one predictable end point that is the same for everyone. Here are some examples of such overstructured activities and some open-ended alternatives:

Overstructured Activity	Open-Ended Alternative
Water table with fourteen items, half of which sink and half of which float, with two trays labeled "Sink" and "Float" for children to sort onto.	Water table with items that sink and float, containers of various sizes to fill and pour from, with and without spouts, and with and without measuring marks on the sides, tubing to pour through, funnels, etc. Children experiment, try things, and ask 100 questions (maybe some are about sinking and floating). The floor is a swamp that they clean up.
Block area dedicated to an activity to use blocks to spell out the letters in your name on the floor.	Following an introduction to the different block shapes and the ways they can be combined (e.g., four quarter circles make a whole solid circle; four half arches make an open circle), begin to point out shapes and letters you see in children's block constructions.

Overstructured Activity	Open-Ended Alternative
Each child gets a sheet of dark blue construction paper with a silhouette of a bare tree drawn on it in black marker. They can glue small white collage scraps or cotton balls on it to make a winter scene.	White, dark blue, and black construction paper are offered to children, with white and black paint and black and white scraps of tissue paper for gluing. They are encouraged to look outside at the snowy day and create an image of what winter looks like or feels like to them. If they ask for related materials (e.g., brown paint or pale blue tissue), they are provided (within reason). Teachers say, "Tell me about what you made," rather than, "What is that?" or "That's so pretty!"

Basic Tools

Enthusiasm for Big Ideas. The alternative to quashing children's "impossible" plans is to enthusiastically support and engage in them. I invite you to think about it for a moment. Is there any harm in *trying* to build a rocket to fly to the moon? #benewbebrave!

You won't achieve that end goal, to be sure (or maybe you will and that's in the big realm of stuff we don't know we don't know), but—oh, my goodness!—even if you don't launch that rocket to the moon, how much will you all learn as you try? I know—I haven't a single clue how to begin either. That's the joy of teaching with fives; we get to discover it all together! You, as the teacher, don't have to know anything except where to find answers and how to organize the process of research into active learning.

Higher Perspective. Young children see everything in the microcosm, the tiny world of me and mine, here and now. Teachers can be their higher perspective. You can bring them some of the macrocosm they're ready to understand or, at least, are ready to explore.

For example, the children report recurring fights in the block area, with conflicts between those who like to use long blocks to create support beams for second- or third-story heights and those who like to lay long blocks out as "fences," space containment for their building area. There are only so many long blocks, and there is only so much floor space.

For the higher perspective, perhaps you introduce *The Butter Battle Book* by Dr. Seuss, which is about respecting differences. Perhaps you help children generalize from the specific by inviting discussions of parallel situations. "What if there were only ten hard-boiled eggs but there were fifteen people to eat? Would we say it's okay for some people to have four or five eggs, like we're saying some people can have a lot of long blocks? How can we be fairer about long blocks?" Caution: Be ready for "buy more long blocks" as one solution. Yay! Fundraising project for the kids!

You could also take the direction of introducing books, images, guest speakers, or walks to nearby construction sites as resources to learn about how foundations are built and building sites protected. Then open a community conversation about how these experiences from the larger world apply to the block area and see where it takes the classroom community.

Big Listening and Careful Mirroring. Part of our #slowdowntunein strategy with this age group is to vastly expand our listening. We must seek to understand more by paring down our teacher-talk. In this case, you can #benewbebrave by asking simple, open-ended questions rather than talking, explaining, and teaching. Repeat what the children say;

mirror them and then extend a bit. In these ways, we support development of language and higher thinking.

> **Frieda:** This red crayon is fire in the fireplace.
> **Teacher:** Mmmm. Fire in the fireplace. That makes the room warm.
> **Frieda:** Yes, warm as warm…warm as…
> **Teacher:** Warm as toast.
> **Frieda:** Warm as baby bunnies.
> **Teacher:** Warm as cuddling mommy.
> **Frieda:** Warm as love.
> **Teacher:** Yes. Warm as love.
> *[They lock eyes and smile at each other as they share this moment.]*
> **Teacher:** The fire in the fireplace makes the room as warm as love. *[Shared smile.]*

With this type of questioning, listening, and modeling, imagine the things you'll both learn. Here's another example:

> **Jamal:** The wings on the plane have this shape.
> **Teacher:** That shape is flatter on the bottom but more curved on the top?
> **Jamal:** Yes, that's right. Like a teardrop smashed a little flat on one side.
> **Teacher:** Why is that the right shape for an airplane wing?
> **Jamal:** I'm not sure, but something about lift.
> **Teacher:** What is lift?
> **Suzie:** It's how air moves to pick the plane up off the ground.
> **Teacher:** How does that work?
> **Suzie:** Ummm…
> **Pearl:** We don't know. Nobody does. Sci-tists don't even agree about it! But airplane wings AND bird wings are all shaped like this to make it lift off the ground. I know that because my dad told me! He

parks planes at the hairport! Ha-ha, that's our joke that we call it that. Hairport! *[all laugh]*

Scaffolded Support. You know scaffolding, right? It's that wonderful assist to construction, built from the ground up and added to as needed to go higher. Construction workers first build the scaffold around where the church spire or high-rise tower will be, then build the spire or tower inside the space contained by the scaffolding.

Great teachers build a scaffold of learning opportunities, always adding new height just beyond children's current understanding, conceptual development, or ability to express their thoughts and feelings. That platform of opportunity offers a hand-up to an eager learner. If the child is truly ready, they will reach up and grasp the new information or concept, grappling with it until their thinking accommodates this bit of disequilibrium. If they are not ready, then the child will simply not see the opportunity as an opportunity. No harm, no foul! Teacher simply builds a platform of opportunity a little less high, or off to the side in a different direction, and tries again.

As children plan and then pursue early implementation of their Big Ideas, they engage in comparing, decision-making, hypothesis testing, and brainstorming. In all these processes within the executive functions (e.g., flexible thinking, working memory, planning and prioritizing, task initiation), teachers play a crucial role. We provide opportunities for little steps upward from where the children seem to be in their capacities for these functions. Those opportunities are tailored for #thischildthismoment and informed by the child's next response, and the next one, for additional attunement.

Documentation. Mirroring the children's processes back to them strengthens their mining of the Vision Treasure. Reflecting back to them, in photos and words, their own process steps and stages of thinking creates shared memories of a community experience that can be talked about for months to come.

As children become more familiar with documentation, they can join in as documenters. We can teach scientific drawing, exact representation for the purpose of documentation. Meanwhile, children are also empowered to experiment with various art media and develop their own visual languages that express how they are making meaning of our world.

Artful teachers also use children's words to describe and ascribe meaning to these drawings, sculptures, and paintings, acknowledging them as external expressions of their internal processes. Children dictate and we transcribe. *Oscar said, "This house has walls all brown inside. It is the brownie house." Then he laughed hard.* Or children write at the level they can—such as a sign reading, "Du Nat Tej Mi Legos ~Jeannie"—and we serve as their translators if necessary (with their guidance, of course!).

For more information on documentation, consider reading this overview by the National Association for the Education of Young Children: https://www.naeyc.org/sites/default/files/globally-shared/downloads/PDFs/resources/pubs/seitz.pdf. A wonderful summary of the purposes of classroom documentation can be found in this blog post by The Compass School, a Reggio Emilia–inspired school with locations in three states: https://www.thecompassschool.com/blog/power-documentation-reggio-inspired-classroom/.

Release to Compromise

Now We Are Six. (I had to; I'm a devoted Winnie-the-Pooh fan.) By six years of age, children's Maturation driver has become

Compromise
Maturation driver—Intimacy
Construction driver—Do I belong?

the desire to have deeper, multilayered, authentic relationships. They are ready to move beyond simply getting what they want. Now they realize they must figure out how to also help others get what *they* want. Even at this young age, we can begin to integrate Trust with the boundaries of Independence, our Faith in the impossible, our capacity for Negotiation, and our aptitude for Vision and planning.

All the Treasures begin to work in concert now, as the Little Red House of personality is almost completely constructed. We have the foundation, side walls, and both slopes of our little triangle roof once Compromise is mined and added to our infrastructure.

Compromise is all about the intimacy of real connection from an authentic self. At six, we need to know if we can connect with others fully. Can I be all of myself—good, bad, and ugly—and still be accepted, welcomed, and loved? Sixes want to know, *Can I belong, even though I'm not perfect?*

This sixth Treasure is about our willingness to find common ground without compromising our essential self, to seek shared understandings without abandoning core beliefs, and to build relationships from those places of intersection. This is the age at which we first learn to welcome and embrace all the amazing diversity of life, actively engaging with it as a great source of adventure and learning.

This is also the age at which we first have the capacity for humility, when we can first, as Rumi wrote, "humble ourselves in the arms of the wild." The "wild" manifests at age six in the wide-ranging creativity of the whole universe, finally laid out in a feast for our eyes, ears, and minds.

Now is when children can truly release their hold on the "rightness" of their story of the world. At six, we can help them discover that there are as many perspectives on the world as there are people in the world. This is the age at which we can learn to be excited, rather than overwhelmed or afraid, as we face that infinite, unknowable diversity.

Broken Tools

Everyone's a Winner. Our most Broken Tool at age six, I fear, grew out of the "I Am Me, I Am Special" movement of the mid-1980s for early childhood environments. (Most humbly, I apologize for my participation. I did the best I could back then with what I knew.) At the age of six, each child should be empowered to own their unique mix of strengths and growing edges—to self-affirm who they are, fully, in all their dimensions—and to accept this same mix of greatness and foibles in others.

Instead, "Special Me" curriculums and their latest ripple effect—a winner's ribbon for everyone—are a setup for children to need constant external validation to feel good about themselves. Knowing in their secret heart, *as we all do*, the petty meanness, jealousy, and feelings of incompetence that are also part of who they are, they feel "wrong" or "less than" even as we affirm their specialness.

Imagine believing that nobody else shares your self-doubt, your jealousy, or your other bits of darkness. Perhaps you know how it feels to keep silent, wishing you were as good as others seem to think you are. I don't believe children hear that they're special when everyone is special. I believe children hear they've been incorrectly included inside the sparkling bubble of "special." They know themselves—better than anyone, after all—and are quite sure they're not 100 percent special. Instead, they feel alone, hiding the secret that they don't belong.

Maybe they become a teenager who guns down classmates. Maybe they take their own life in a desperate act after just twenty-four years. Maybe they simply become an angry, fearful, or unhappy adult, struggling to find a place they feel at home in the skin of who they really are. They eat too much, drink too much, watch too much TV, gamble their money away, or fill their life with toys, play, and partying. Let's not set up kids for these kinds of feelings, resulting from the backlash of an overfocus on "special."

Judging Other. A corollary of overvalidating a child's specialness is to make the "other" wrong, whomever that Other may be. If *we* are special, then it does follow that anything that goes wrong must be the fault of the Other. Did a child fight with another child in their neighborhood? To affirm the goodness, the heroic specialness, of this child before us, we must cast that Other child as villain.

Perhaps we shift the villain role upward, using a story of bad parents or poor upbringing. One version of this approach comes at teachers from the direction of parents. Their child can't be bad—they're a little angel at home—so the teacher must be the problem. Sound familiar?

A beloved friend of mine tells of how her mother taught her to examine her own role in any upset, discord, or misunderstanding. I've seen teachers hold children similarly responsible; it is part of owning our personal authority, after all. Choice, Agency, *and* Responsibility take us into relationships. Children need to understand and discuss their roles in interpersonal ripples and rifts. The Broken Tool of Judging Other shifts all the blame away from #thischildthismoment. We rob the child of their reality, thinking we're protecting them by absolving them of blame and erasing the pain of guilt.

Yet they still feel the distress of whatever discord occurred. Deep in their hearts, they know they are not blameless. They may conclude they are as villainous as the Other, who was judged at fault. This Broken Tool can leave a child wondering if we'd still love and respect them if we knew their secret heart.

Basic Tools

To support a child's Treasure mining work at this age, remember that what now drives Maturation is the need for intimacy, and Construction seeks the answer to, "Do I belong?" Compromise, as a Childhood Treasure, allows a child to elevate "getting along in the sandbox" to the next level.

However, it also asks them to face the paradox that, as they learn to be themselves in a more complex social community, the stakes are higher. The heart of intimacy is being vulnerable enough to be seen. Children must allow others the privilege of "into-me-see" (i.e., inti-ma-cy). They must learn how to safely express the person contained inside their boundaries as well as to cope with the consequences of being *seen* in all their glorious, messy authenticity in a world often brimming with judgment.

Teachers can help children face these external forces by reminding them of their boundaries and sharing their adult certainty that each child is supposed to be a unique individual. Affirm that people being different from each other is as normal as trees and flowers and animals being different from each other. Teachers are the voice for, "Of course you're different! You're supposed to be."

FWT—Feel, Want, Think. KWL is a well-known teaching tool in The Project Approach in which we ask the children to tell us what they **K**now and **W**ant to know about a new topic and then, after a learning project, to tell us what they **L**earned. The **FWT** tool for mining the Treasure of Compromise uses a similar brainstorming approach.

With teacher guidance, children who are in conflict learn to ask each other these three questions: "What emotion do you **F**eel right now? What do you **W**ant? What do you **T**hink we should do?" Let's say that a Reading and Writing Circle of five children all nearing seven years of age, who call themselves The Literacy Jedi, are having a disagreement about a plot direction in a play they are writing together. They pause from their writing work to build community with FWT and create a chart that looks like this:

Literacy Jedi:	Feels	Wants	Thinks
Marquis	~~Tired~~ Bored	Action	Take a nap
Jennilee	Confused	Action	Take a stretch break
Opal	Angry	Romance	Punch Noland
Noland	Confused	Action	Get a snack
Tayanna	Bored	Action AND Romance	Have both

NOTE: After Marquis said he felt "tired," Jennilee questioned whether that was an emotion.

The whole group got excited about Tayanna's idea to have the next plot direction be *both* action and romance rather than choosing one over the other. However, the teacher encouraged them to review and discuss the whole FWT chart before going on with their writing to better understand their group process. The continued conversation gave Opal a chance to discharge her anger at Noland in a healthy way, with words.

Marquis had an insight and wondered whether the boredom or confusion the rest of the group were all feeling, and their desire to take a break, might have been escapes from the anger they could see building in Opal's body language and tone of voice. Noland concluded their FWT review when he rested a gentle hand on Opal's shoulder, smiled, and said, "Next time you get mad at me, tell me before you want to punch me, okay?"

Of course, children will not be this adept at the FWT process immediately upon turning six or the first time you introduce it. This tool is a sophisticated one and requires repeated exposure and practice with guidance. Over time, children can become capable of independent conversations. They will do so more easily if all the other five Treasures before Compromise have been well mined and used to build a sturdy Little Red House.

Commonalty Commons. When a piece of land is designated as a "Commons," it is shared as a resource belonging to the whole community. Other resources can also be held in common in a community. For this Basic Tool, dedicate some wall space or whiteboard space to create a place for sharing your group's common ground. This tool allows a classroom community to see the experiences and strengths they share in common.

Using tools such as markers on a whiteboard, index cards and double-stick tape or a sticky wall, or sticky notes on cardboard, children share aspects of their lives, their dislikes and likes, or the ways in which they feel capable. Other children show they share that common ground with a symbol or their initials. A Commonalty Commons might look like this:

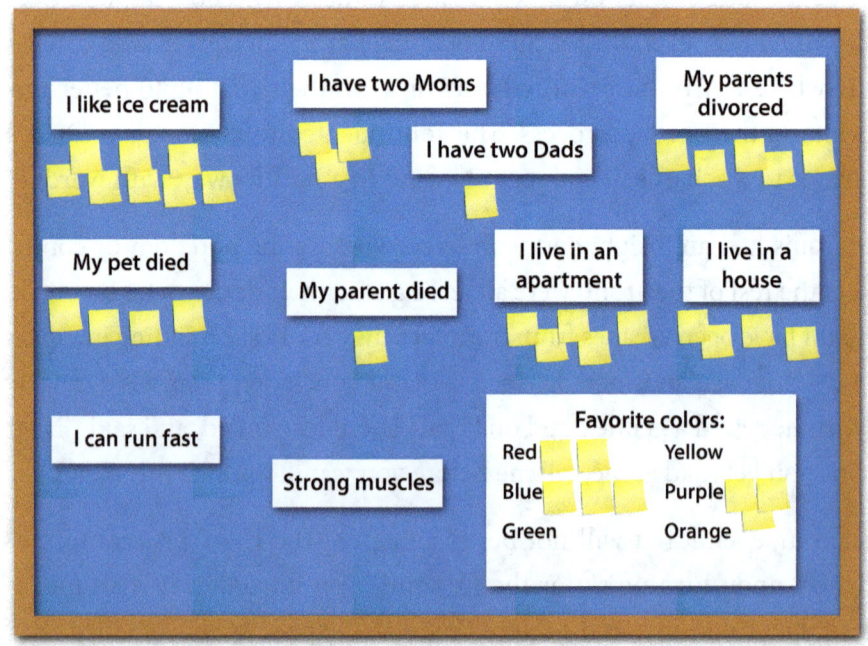

As with so many activities in classrooms for this age, your group can design the process. With your input and guidance, they can decide the Limits and Agreements that "govern" this space. For example, one classroom might agree to show who connects to each characteristic, with names or symbols for each child, while another group makes it all anonymous.

(**A sidebar:** As they talk over the rules of the game, encourage them to provide their rationales: Why anonymous? Why use names? What is the intention? Teachers who encourage such reflection and sharing support children's strong desire at this age to learn both persuasion and discernment through practice in a safe place. Children are bombarded with massive amounts of persuasive input by this age. No longer the innocent and gullible children who believe everything adults tell them, they crave tools to help sort the mental wheat from the chaff. Let them "call B.S." on each other in some agreed-upon, gentle way to ask for clarity on a point of view. Children need to learn when and how to say, "That doesn't make sense to me," or "Your argument is not convincing me.")

As children develop more skill and responsibility in their use of your community's tools for the Commons, they will also develop more comfort with the *concept* of finding common ground with others. As they do, your class may want to play with or tweak their start-up approach. For example, your Commons rules may change a bit, by group agreement. Or, perhaps for a month, the Commons becomes a place to share goals, then successes the next month. Then in another month, the focus shifts to family structure or experience with animals or any number of topics.

Sixes can also begin to discover how this shared knowledge ripples into all areas of community life. While planning the order in a relay race, we might hear, "Luisa and Joey, the Commons says you are also good at running, right?" Over time, children's sophistication will continue to grow as they use the Commons. Over time, they build a classroom community in which each child is recognized for their strengths and treated with compassion for losses and other challenges.

Don't fall into the "teach empathy" trap. Not even the most gifted teacher can *teach* empathy. Nobody can. Yet all of us can transform ourselves into someone who can encourage it, help it grow, shine a light on it, and make it visible to children. Remember, the availability of these Childhood Treasures is part of our hardwiring from birth. The opportunity to mine them arises with each new pair of drivers for Maturation and Construction. Teaching and Learning opportunities provide the right mining tools in a time of readiness. Nothing we do provides the raw ore. It's there from day one.

Persistence via Acceptance

Finally, at seven years, Maturation is driven by the need to sustain effort, to persevere, through challenges. The light of logical

Acceptance
Maturation driver—Perseverance
Construction driver—Can I thrive through change?

thinking first dawns at six to seven years of age, allowing the child to see better how the world works. As children move fully beyond the magical thinking of the three and four, they begin to understand cause and effect and to see the reversibility of most actions, which they could not see before.

Piaget, the Swiss epistemologist and developmental psychologist, developed and researched our early understanding of concrete logic in young children. Before logic, children do not understand that changing the appearance of something doesn't change its nature. They do not understand that a person in a costume and makeup is still the person they know rather than the being they appear to be. They do not understand that creating more space between the pennies in a row, causing the line to be longer, doesn't make it more pennies. So many things that adults simply take for granted, they do not see and cannot understand yet in their prelogical state.

There's nothing wrong; it's a stage of development, intended to come to an end. As with other transitions in development, its ending can be seen in external behavior. Logic emerges in the wake of a rather substantial reorganization of the central nervous system that also helps define the physical midline separating right from left. So, teachers of seven-year-olds can witness the disappearance of mirror-image writing and be present for the birth of finally knowing the right hand from the left, both of which ride in on the maturational coattails of logic.

Once logical, at least on the physical plane if not in the abstract, seven-year-olds finally "get" that change is not always permanent and, in fact, not always true change. Diversity of experience (aka "change") begins to look like a potential partner in life, something to dance with rather than a mystical occurrence we must endure. Children of this age can begin to understand how to live with change as a daily fact and still move successfully along a path of intention toward goals. They learn that they can still, through the rise and fall of circumstances, get what they want, have their needs met, express who they are, and pursue their dreams and big plans.

By seven, the brain is as fully wired as it's ever going to be. Now, every interaction sends electricity zinging along some barely laid connection or a pathway already deeply carved. Each firing of each synapse strengthens that connection.

The neural network is now being used to support continued construction of understanding and meaning. The structure and diversity in this network were built from birth to about five years. Now it either fosters or limits the child's internal life—thought, emotion, and aspiration—and the outward physical expression of that life.

It's time to learn that every challenge is not an insurmountable barrier. What if young children could emerge into middle childhood feeling positively about change and its impact on their lives? What if they could see themselves as surfing the waves of change in their lives rather than drowning under them? What if they knew that the gift of their uniquely created and creative inner world is worth carrying through storm, fire, and flood? What if they knew they'd be strengthened by this universal journey?

Broken Tools

Mother Maxims. In truth, I don't know whether we adults trot out our little sound bites to describe life from a negative frame more often for children of this age. I do believe this is the age at which they finally start to hear them and find their brains are already wired up around these bon mots. Here are…well, I started with a few but quickly wrote several:

- Life's no picnic!
- You can't fight city hall.
- Whatever.
- Life's a b*tch and then you die.
- It doesn't matter.
- Nice guys finish last.
- Who cares, really?
- There's nothing you can do about it.
- You have to fight for everything you want.
- Same old, same old!
- Let it roll off you, like water off a duck's back. (My mom's personal favorite.)
- Learn to live with it.
- Just let it go.

The last three come closest to one of the Basic Tools, Surfing Safari. However, without the addition of honoring the child's feelings and a few teaching conversations, even these instructions don't help much. Many children listen to the adults in their lives repeat such statements regularly. Even if the adults at home and school do not, there are adults on TV and YouTube and out in the wider world these children increasingly inhabit: store clerks, coaches, youth mentors, teens in their neighborhood.

Fighting What Is. Sometimes it's difficult to catch ourselves doing this one, it's such a habitual pattern. The objective description is this: Whatever is occurring around us, whatever set of circumstances is prevailing in the day, it raises our ire or starts us whining. Whether we react with anger or feeling put-upon, our verbiage decries that what *IS* should not be.

Yet, it still is. Rejecting what is or pontificating on why it's wrong, crying foul, or yelling makes not one whit of difference in the set of circumstances before us. There they still are, whenever our rant winds down.

Throughout their day and all the venues in which they move, children see adults literally rant and rail against reality. A more familiar term for this behavior is complaining. What version of this might occur in a classroom relationship between teachers and seven-year-old students? How about:

- You boys need to STOP running around and come sit down; we're reading a book now.
- Children, you are NOT putting the caps back on the markers, and they are drying out!
- Jumping into the beanbag from there is NOT okay!
- [Kids overhearing two teachers talking] They just CAN'T increase our work days without compensating us better!

- Why CAN'T you kids remember to check in your weekend activity bags?
- Who keeps mixing up all the pattern cards? Why CAN'T you be responsible with our things?

What else have you complained about this week? Fighting with what IS manifests in other statements and behavior, but it can always be identified by three key features of its essential nature: 1) it remarks upon what is wrong, 2) it comes from a framework of assigning blame, and 3) it offers no real solution beyond the offender ceasing the action.

Basic Tools

Beautiful Elephant. If children are to honor and elevate their birthright capacity for persevering through challenge—what I call mining the Treasure of Acceptance—they need to face change. We must help them look change squarely in the face and say, "Well, okay then." We need to talk openly and honestly about the "elephant in the living room" that everyone sees but none acknowledge. Our culture has some Mother Maxims about how change is the only constant in life, but we rarely integrate the reality of those casual words.

At seven, children need gentle, compassionate support to see the truth that change is the only constant in life. They need our help to see this big elephant of a truth filling ALL the room in which we live, no matter where we are. Change is here, always, and ever will be. Of that fundamental fact of life, there can be no reasonable doubt. So, if we want children to see that change is nothing to fear and is simply a natural part of life—even a beautiful part—then let us show it to them. Let us name the elephant and study it. Let us see deeply into its complex beauty.

Nature is a great place to begin. In your science area, you have basic botany, zoology, chemistry, and physics, just for starters, to explore natural change processes. The metamorphosis of a tadpole to a frog or a caterpillar to a butterfly, the interaction of flour with several wet ingredients when heat is applied, a lima bean sprouting its green glory in a paper cup full of potting soil, all reveal that change is everywhere in nature.

Go outside and observe the changing seasons, however they occur where you live. How much rain or snow do you get each month? How does the temperature vary? How much cloud cover is there day by day? How does your local watershed change with the snowmelt or summer's drought? What kinds of trees surround you, and how do they change over the course of a year? You, teacher, don't need to know the answers. You only need the willingness to explore the questions.

These lessons about change provide a natural platform to talk about how humans change: our bodies grow, we learn to walk and talk, we get some hair, we get some teeth, then lose them and get new teeth. Learning about our physical changes flows seamlessly into learning about how we change in other ways: in skills and knowledge, opinions, and emotions. What we value in a friend changes over time, and our plans for our future life shift. The Big Dreams we dream transform over time, as do our needs in relationships.

Now *this* is a Social Studies learning experience worth sharing with your community of children! But no formal lesson plans need to be written. All of this can be explored in authentic conversation with children at opportune, teachable moments, whenever a mental field is ready for a seed. In response to some common comments we hear from sevens, how different are the responses below compared to those you have given in the past?

Child: Fontana and Majique won't let me sit with them.

Teacher: Is that a big change or a small change from how it usually is?

Child: I can ride my bike without training wheels now!

Teacher: How does the change in balancing skills feel in your body?

Child: I want to make a new label for my locker. I don't like purple so much anymore.

Teacher: Well, sure, and that's an interesting change! You *really* liked purple! Do you have a new favorite color?

Child: Mommy and Daddy told me and my sisters last night we're moving in a month to another house far away.

Teacher: That is a very big change in your lives. And it will be a change for all of us here too. I'm glad we have a month to talk about that and share our feelings. Do you want to tell the rest of our class today or wait until Monday?

Child: My Mommy and Daddy are gone, and now I live with Grandma.

Teacher: Your grandma told me that mommy and daddy are in prison now, and you will visit them there sometimes. These are some very big changes in your life. I'm here to listen if you want to talk, and I can help support you when you're ready to talk about it with the other friends in our community.

Seeing the beauty in the ubiquitous elephant called Change asks you, teacher, to #benewbebrave and #staysanebeyourself. We must let go of the patterned, habitual kinds of responses we give children when they are faced with changes large and small. Children need you to find the courage to be authentic with them, to be present to their experience, no matter what you learned about change when you were their age. To do that requires you to mine your own Treasures and cultivate a S.E.L.F.

Surfing Safari. Acknowledging change as life's true constant suggests a second metaphor for another Basic Tool: the constant ebb and flow of the tide. In the ocean of life, we teachers help children learn to ride the waves of change rather than be overwhelmed and knocked off their emotional and spiritual feet by this natural and regularly occurring force.

In any of the examples above, where the teacher found ways to show that change is a natural part of our beautiful lives, the conversation might evolve to include some surfing strategies. Teachers can ask children to reflect on the change at hand, whatever it may be, in a variety of ways.

For each of the scenarios above, here's one possible follow-up question to add as the conversation continues (assume this is not the very next thing the teacher says, but that a dialogue occurs into which this second question fits seamlessly):

Child: Fontana and Majique won't let me sit with them today.

- **Teacher:** Is that a big change or a small change from how it usually is?
- **Teacher:** Think back…can you remember something that happened to upset your friendship?

Child: I can ride my bike without training wheels now!

- **Teacher:** How does the change in balancing skills feel in your body?
- **Teacher:** What other activities can you do because your balance is stronger?

Child: I want to make a new label for my locker. I don't like purple so much anymore.

- **Teacher:** Well, sure, and that's an interesting change! You *really* liked purple! Do you have a new favorite color?
- **Teacher:** How did you first notice purple wasn't your favorite color anymore?

Child: Mommy and Daddy told me and my sisters last night we're moving in a month to another house far away.

- **Teacher:** That is a very big change in your lives. And it will be a change for all of us here too. I'm glad we have a month to talk about that and share our feelings. Do you want to tell the rest of our class today or wait until Monday?
- **Teacher:** Are there friends here you want to stay in touch with, and how might you do that?

Child: My mommy and daddy are gone, and now I live with Grandma.

- **Teacher:** Your grandma told me that Mommy and Daddy are in prison now, and you will visit them there sometimes. These are some very big changes in your life. I'm here to listen if you want to talk, and I can help support you when you're ready to talk about it with the other friends in our community.
- **Teacher:** What are some things that will be different at Grandma's house? (Help them think of things like bed, where the bathroom is, food at meals, different yard to play in.)

Reflecting on the change, noticing the features of a new landscape, and talking about them helps make the change itself feel more manageable for children. Begin with reflections on the what—the physical nature of the change—before adding questions about thoughts and feelings, needs and dreams.

Recall the Change. This is an activity to offer the classroom community. Your whole class can engage in it together, or small groups can begin the work and later bring their thinking together with that of other small groups in a whole-class discussion.

The objective is to create a group-recalled history of your time together through the lens of *What has changed?* Create a disc, perhaps simply a circle drawn on a big sheet of paper or cut out of cardboard and affixed to a base so that it turns. Maybe create a time line on a whiteboard. Get as fancy or as basic as you like because the conversation is the real point!

Mark a spot on the time line or wheel rim as a starting point (a date or event, such as the first day of the school year). Ask the children to remember what they and the classroom were like at that point. Ask open questions such as: What did we know back then? How did we act? What did the room look like? What was the weather like outside? Select another point on the wheel to represent an event a few weeks later, such as Back-to-School Night. How had we changed by then? Did we know anything new? Did we act differently? Had the weather changed? What about our classroom; has it changed? How?

As children get older and better at recalling change, you might also add a "predict the future" part of this activity. Imagine it is the last day of school. What might we know then that we don't know now? How might we act in new ways by then? How else might we change before the end of the year? Let children be aspirational about how change may transform them and the community of your classroom.

Educating in the Little Red House

Is this book a curriculum? No. *Let the Child Shine* offers two sets of strategies for teachers to consider in the context of a new framework for fostering social and emotional development. I'm not sure how commonplace it is, but I've received performance appraisal feedback with this kind of approach of "stop doing these things" and "continue or start doing these things." So, this book could be considered an opportunity to perform a self-assessment.

Lining up all the Maturation drivers, Construction drivers, and Basic Tools does not make a curriculum. What this book does is say, "Stop handing these Broken Tools to children" and "Start or continue handing these Basic Tools to children and refine your skills with them." Consider *Let the Child Shine* a guide toward a new pedagogy for social and emotional development. As *the method and practice of teaching*, your pedagogy expresses your internal philosophy. Your pedagogy is the external evidence of your internal understanding, just as children's behavior expresses their understanding.

I hope I've given you a new understanding, using the mental models and teaching story of the ***7 Childhood Treasures***, the Little Red House of personality, and the Choice-Agency-Responsibility mobile for traveling into relationships. As you gain in courage and open your natural curiosity to each uniquely sparkling child, you will discover all they can do.

Let us all STOP calling insightful, funny, intelligent children Cuh-YOOT and using the strategies of the Anti-Sparkle Plan. Let us all put down the Broken Tools of the past. To replace these Broken Tools, let us START or CONTINUE our generosity in handing out these Basic Tools for each of the ***7 Childhood Treasures*** ready to be mined:

Childhood Treasure	Maturation Driver	Construction Driver	Basic Mining Tools
Trust	Physical independence	Will my needs be met?	• Respond…Even to Silence • Mirror • Return the Serve
Independence	Autonomy	What is me/not me?	• Emo Lingo • Emo Express • Showing the Impact • How Does It Feel?

Childhood Treasure	Maturation Driver	Construction Driver	Basic Mining Tools
Faith	Initiative; Big Dreams	Can I believe in myself?	• Optimum Flexibility • The Answer to How Is Yes
Negotiation	Law and order	Can I get along with others?	• Clear Communication • Community Meetings • Community-Created Rules • Peace Chairs/Mats • Teach Competition
Vision	Competence	Can I learn and "become"?	• Enthusiasm for Big Ideas • Higher Perspective • Big Listening and Careful Mirroring • Scaffolded Support • Documentation
Compromise	Intimacy	Do I belong?	• FWT—Feel, Want, Think • Commonalty Commons
Acceptance	Perseverance	Can I thrive through change?	• Beautiful Elephant • Surfing Safari • Recall the Change

You may be thinking that children must learn a great deal other than the answers to these seven Construction drivers on your watch as their teacher. That is certainly true. Yet if they cannot learn to manage themselves in relationships with others, they will acquire little else in any future learning environment because all such environments include relationships. If they can learn to manage themselves in relationships with others, through the mining of these *7 Childhood Treasures*, then this foundation of social and emotional development gives them the freedom to learn everything else.

Conclusion

As a teacher for children in the midst of mining the **7 Childhood Treasures**, I know you see their importance. You are already aware that social and emotional development has proven the most important factor in school success. This book, I hope, gives you a mental model for supporting that development through attention to these seven interpersonal assets.

At seven years of age, from the solid shelter of a Little Red House built by mining the Treasures, you could have seen the promise of your whole life before you. All the possibilities that you were back then might have stood, poised and ready to drive your Choice-Agency-Responsibility mobile into the many relationships of life. If that doesn't sound like you at seven, that's okay. It's never too late to go mining for those gems because the raw ores remain, waiting for your attention.

I hope you also see the importance of some Development Do-Overs for yourself. Secure the corners of your own Little Red House first before helping children build theirs, just as you'd secure your oxygen mask first in a flight emergency. When your own **7 Childhood Treasures** are gleaming in every junction of your Little Red House, and your C.A.R. is gassed up with Choice, Agency, and personal Responsibility and ready to roll, you can be confident in your support for the little miners in your classroom.

I encourage every teacher to "Shine!" You shine first so you can **Let the Child Shine!**

About the Author

Dr. L. Carol Scott is an expert in the education of young children, from birth through age seven. Also teaching other teachers to see the full potential in children is her delight and passion now, for more than 30 years. Her experience working in or with settings as varied as university laboratory preschools, family child care, and public school K–2 classrooms, fills her work with rich examples of real kids and teachers.

Along with her professional education and experience with thousands of children, parents and teachers, you benefit from Dr. Scott's personal experience. As she achieved an MA in Early Childhood Education, PhD in Developmental and Child Psychology, and a prominent career, Dr. Scott also pursued her own psychological wholeness following a childhood full of Adverse Childhood Experiences. Into that professional mastery she has woven a hard-won emotional intelligence, a wide and embracing empathy, and a deep understanding of what creates and sustains healthy relationships for adults. Using her *7 Childhood Treasures* approach, her own Development Do-Overs supported her recovery from trauma in her early years. As one proof point for the power of the work she offers, she shares the story of her recovery, using the wisdom of early childhood development.

Dr. Scott provides keynote addresses, workshops, seminars, online and college courses, and leadership for the future of human development… your development.

www.ingramcontent.com/pod-product-compliance
Lightning Source LLC
Chambersburg PA
CBHW052036070526
44584CB00016B/2071